ATLAS OF CONFLICTS

WORLD WAR II:

EUROPE

Reg Grant

W
FRANKLIN WATTS
LONDON•SYDNEY

Titles in this series:

THE ARAB-ISRAELI CONFLICT
THE KOREAN WAR
THE VIETNAM WAR
WORLD WAR I
WORLD WAR II: EUROPE
WORLD WAR II: THE PACIFIC

© 2004 Arcturus Publishing

Produced for Franklin Watts by Arcturus Publishing
Ltd, 26/27 Bickels Yard, 151-153 Bermondsey Street,
London SE1 3HA.

Series concept: Alex Woolf
Editor: Philip de Ste. Croix
Designer: Simon Borrough
Cartography: The Map Studio
Consultant: Paul Cornish, Imperial War Museum,
  London
Picture researcher: Thomas Mitchell

Published in the UK by Franklin Watts.

A CIP catalogue record for this book is available from
the British Library.

ISBN 0 7496 5447 3

Printed and bound in Italy

Franklin Watts – the Watts Publishing Group,
96 Leonard Street, London EC2A 4XD.

Picture Acknowledgements:
All the photographs in this book were supplied by
Getty Images and are reproduced here with their
permission.

ABOUT THE AUTHOR

The author, Reg Grant, studied history at the
University of Oxford, and is the author of more than a
dozen books on modern history. He specializes in the
history of the twentieth century. His book *The
Holocaust* (1997) was shortlisted for the *Times
Educational Supplement*'s Senior Information Book
Award.

CONTENTS

CHAPTER 1: THE WAR BEGINS

German dictator Adolf Hitler shakes hands with army officers at a Nazi Party rally in 1934. Hitler rapidly expanded Germany's armed forces through the 1930s.

World War II is generally said to have started on 1 September 1939, when Germany, ruled by the Nazi dictator Adolf Hitler, invaded its neighbour Poland. But conflict in Europe had been building up for several years before that date.

Hitler had come to power in Germany in 1933. He was publicly committed to the overthrow of the Versailles Treaty, the peace treaty imposed by the victors on a defeated Germany in 1919 at the end of the Great War (now known as World War I). Under the terms of the treaty, Germany was only allowed a small army with limited armaments and no air force. It was not allowed to have troops in the Rhineland, the part of Germany bordering on France. The borders of Germany set by the treaty left many German-speaking people outside the country's frontier. Austria, whose population was mostly German-speaking, was forbidden to become part of Germany.

Hitler challenged the Versailles settlement step-by-step. He rapidly set about rebuilding Germany's armed forces, including its air force. Rearmament was already well under way by the time it was officially announced in 1935. The following year German troops marched into the demilitarized Rhineland. Britain and France, the two powers mainly responsible for the Versailles Treaty and with a major interest in upholding it, protested but did nothing.

THE AXIS ALLIANCE In 1936 Hitler formed the Axis alliance with another dictator, Italy's Benito Mussolini, who had angered Britain and France in 1935 by his invasion of the independent African country of Abyssinia (Ethiopia). When civil war broke out in Spain in July 1936, Germany and Italy sent military forces to support General Francisco Franco's Nationalist rebels against the Republican government. Franco eventually triumphed in 1939.

Meanwhile, emboldened by his success in remilitarizing the Rhineland, in March 1938 Hitler annexed Austria – this was known as the Anschluss ('joining together'). Hitler's army faced no resistance and he was greeted by cheering crowds in the Austrian capital, Vienna. Once again, Britain and France did nothing.

Next Hitler's attention turned to Czechoslovakia, a well-armed democratic country and an ally of France. Czechoslovakia had a large German-speaking minority living in the Sudetenland area, bordering on Germany. Hitler threatened to invade Czechoslovakia to 'liberate' the Sudeten Germans. This seemed certain to lead to war with Britain and France. But in September 1938, at a conference held in Munich, Britain and France agreed to join with Germany and Italy in ordering the Czechs to hand over the Sudetenland to Germany. British prime minister Neville Chamberlain returned

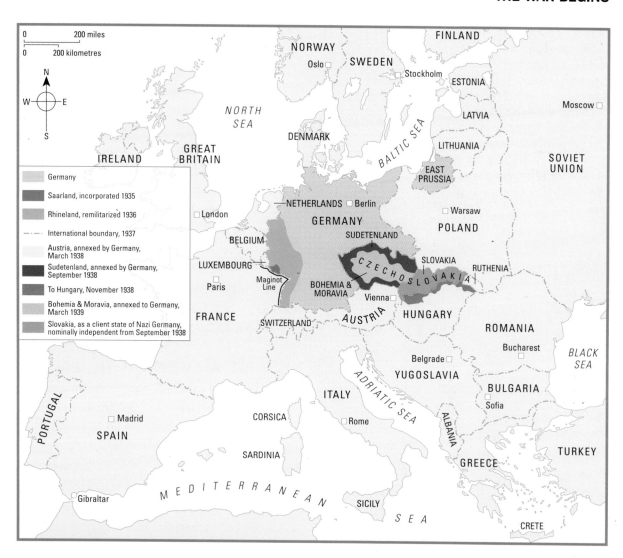

Legend:
- Germany
- Saarland, incorporated 1935
- Rhineland, remilitarized 1936
- ·—·—· International boundary, 1937
- Austria, annexed by Germany, March 1938
- Sudetenland, annexed by Germany, September 1938
- To Hungary, November 1938
- Bohemia & Moravia, annexed to Germany, March 1939
- Slovakia, as a client state of Nazi Germany, nominally independent from September 1938

HITLER'S ACHIEVEMENTS

In April 1939, German Nazi dictator Adolf Hitler looked back triumphantly over his successes. He declared: '*I have … endeavoured to destroy sheet by sheet that Treaty [of Versailles] which … contains the vilest oppression which peoples and human beings have ever been expected to put up with. I have brought back to the Reich provinces stolen from us in 1919; I have led back to their native country millions of Germans who were torn away from us and were in misery…*'

[Quoted in *Hitler*, Joachim Fest]

The Saarland voted to rejoin Germany in 1935. The rest of Germany's expansion was achieved by the threat of military action.

Hitler drives triumphantly through the streets of the Austrian capital, Vienna, after the annexation of Austria – the Anschluss – in June 1938.

Danzig – now Gdansk – on the Baltic provided Hitler with a pretext for invading Poland in September 1939. Once the Soviet Union also invaded from the east, the Poles had no chance. The partition of Poland had secretly been agreed between Germany and the Soviet Union before the war began.

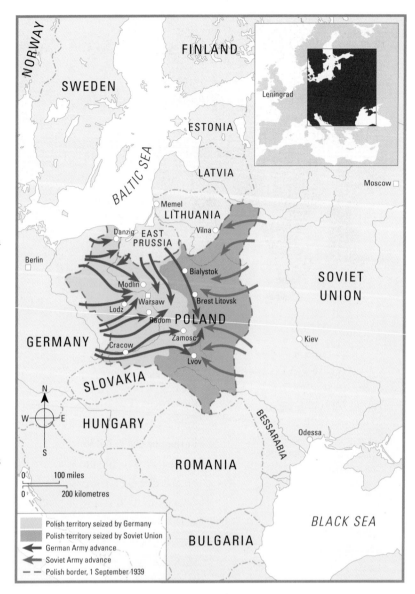

to Britain claiming 'peace with honour', while German forces occupied the Sudetenland without a shot being fired.

Chamberlain and other 'appeasers' believed that if Hitler was allowed to overturn the Versailles Treaty, gathering all German-speaking people within Germany's borders, he would be satisfied and peace would be maintained. But in reality Hitler's ambitions went much further. His ultimate goal, as he told his generals in 1939, was to obtain 'living space [*Lebensraum*] in the East'. This meant that Germany must conquer Slav peoples such as the Czechs, Poles and Russians to create a German-ruled empire that would dominate Europe. This would also allow Hitler to crush other groups he hated and feared, especially communists and Jews.

Hitler had declared the Sudetenland his 'last territorial claim in Europe'. But in March 1939 German troops marched into the Czech capital, Prague, and Czechoslovakia ceased to exist. In the same month, Germany took over Memel on the Baltic and Italy invaded Albania. Then the focus shifted to Poland. The Poles were in dispute with Germany over the port of Danzig (Gdansk). Although it had mainly a German population, the peace treaty had made Danzig a 'Free City' linked to Poland. Hitler demanded the return of Danzig to Germany and a 'corridor' through Poland to link Germany with East Prussia.

THE SOVIET ALLIANCE Now shamed by their failure to defend Czechoslovakia, in April 1939 Britain and France signed a treaty with Poland, committing themselves to go to war if the Poles were attacked. The crucial issue then was the position of the Soviet Union, led by the communist dictator Josef Stalin. The British, French and Polish governments disliked and distrusted Stalin. But in the summer of 1939 Britain and France rather half-heartedly sought an alliance with the Soviet Union, aware that only the Soviets were in a position to give the Poles immediate military assistance in case of a German invasion.

Hitler and Stalin were, on the face of it, implacable enemies. Nazism was an explicitly anti-communist

DEVASTATING DEFEAT

During the fighting in Poland in 1939, the death toll was high and many more were taken prisoner. The estimated figures are:

60,000   Poles killed in action
25,000   Polish civilians killed
694,000 Polish prisoners in German hands
217,000 Polish prisoners in Russian hands

German losses, although substantial, were far lighter:
14,000   German soldiers killed

movement. The Soviets had sent military aid to the Republican side in the Spanish Civil War. Yet in August 1939, while the British and French dithered, Hitler sent a delegation to Russia which swiftly struck a ruthless deal with the Soviets. Publicly this Nazi-Soviet Pact was a non-aggression treaty – an agreement that Nazi Germany and the Soviet Union would not attack one another. But secretly the two powers agreed to partition Poland between them.

On 1 September 1939 German troops invaded Poland. The Poles had a large army, but with out-of-date equipment. Germany, by contrast, used its most modern tank formations and aircraft in the invasion. The tanks moved fast, punching holes in the Polish lines and penetrating deep inside Poland. They were supported by Stuka dive-bombers, acting as 'aerial artillery'. The German *Luftwaffe* (air force) also bombed Polish cities, terrorizing the population.

The Polish forces were already in disarray when, on 17 September, the Soviet Union invaded eastern Poland. The Polish government fled

German soldiers pull down a barrier on the Polish border on 1 September 1939. In response to the invasion of Poland, Britain and France declared war on Germany two days later.

Soviet commisar for foreign affairs Vyacheslav Molotov signs a non-aggression pact with Nazi Germany on 23 August 1939, watched by German foreign minister Joachim von Ribbentrop (left).

the country the next day. Warsaw, the Polish capital, surrendered on 28 September. The defeat of Poland had taken four weeks.

WAR ON GERMANY

The German invasion of Poland led Britain and France to declare war on Germany on 3 September. But the British and French government had no enthusiasm for war and did nothing effective to help the Poles. Britain was in no position to help Poland militarily, and France, which could have launched an offensive against Germany, was committed to a defensive strategy. A British Expeditionary Force was sent to France but the Allied forces stayed on the defensive – even though, with the best German troops occupied in Poland, Germany's western border would have been vulnerable to a swift attack. Once Poland was defeated, Britain and France felt even less inclined to go on the attack.

Finnish soldiers wearing winter camouflage man a machine-gun during the war between Finland and the Soviet Union in 1939-40.

The Finns used troops on skis to launch counter-offensives after the Soviet invasion.

Germany and the Soviet Union duly carved up Poland between them. The Soviet Union also bullied the independent Baltic states, Estonia, Latvia and Lithuania, into allowing Soviet troops to be stationed on their territory. But another of the Soviet Union's neighbours, Finland, was not so accommodating.

The Soviet Union proposed changes to its border with Finland which would have improved the Soviet defensive position in case of an attack from the west. The Finns refused. On 30 November 1939 the Soviet Red Army invaded Finland. To their surprise, they met fierce resistance. In harsh winter weather, over 120,000 Soviet soldiers died attempting to breach the Finnish defences. As Finnish resistance held the

Soviet army at bay, Britain and France discussed sending an expeditionary force to support the Finns – an action which would have put them simultaneously at war with the Soviet Union and Germany.

In February 1940, however, the Red Army broke through and the following month the Finns were forced to accept a peace agreement that gave the Soviet Union rather more territory than it had originally asked for. In the summer of 1940, Stalin went on to absorb Estonia, Latvia and Lithuania into the Soviet Union, and took the province of Bessarabia from Romania. But by then momentous events in Western Europe had distracted attention from the East.

INCAPABLE REDS

The events of the Winter War led many people to underestimate Soviet military strength. In a radio broadcast in January 1940, Winston Churchill, then Britain's First Lord of the Admiralty, said that Finland *'had exposed, for the world to see, the incapacity of the Red Army.'*
[Quoted in *History of the Second World War*, B.H. Liddel Hart]

The Mannerheim Line, a strong defensive position named after Finland's senior military commander, was the key to the war between the Soviet Union and Finland in 1939-40. After the Soviets broke through the Line in February 1940, the Finns soon had to agree to a negotiated peace.

CHAPTER 2:
BLITZKRIEG

The Junkers Ju-87 dive-bomber, known as the Stuka, was a crucial weapon in Germany's 'Blitzkrieg' offensives in the early years of the war.

The period between September 1939 and April 1940 in western Europe was dubbed the 'Phoney War'. The British Expeditionary Force (BEF) in France numbered over 350,000 troops by the spring of 1940, and France had mobilized an army almost five million strong. But there was no significant fighting. The Allied forces passively awaited a German offensive, manning the Maginot Line (see map on page 5), a powerful concrete fortification along France's frontier with Germany that spread out along the border with neutral Belgium.

In April 1940, partly in response to criticism of the lack of military action, Britain and France decided to move to cut off supplies of iron ore that were being exported to Germany from mines in neutral Sweden. The iron ore was being shipped chiefly through Narvik, a port in another neutral country, Norway. On 8 April the Allies sent ships to mine Norwegian coastal waters. They also prepared to land troops at key Norwegian ports.

GERMANS ATTACK NORWAY But the Germans had been planning their own invasion of Norway. On 9 April, German troops seized control of neutral Denmark and moved on to attack Norway. In a series of lightning moves, they occupied coastal

German troops drag a gun up a beach during the Norwegian campaign in the spring of 1940.

towns from Oslo in the south to Narvik in the far north. Airborne troops were parachuted in to capture key airfields – the first use of parachutists in war – but most of the German soldiers arrived by ship.

THE ROYAL NAVY The British Royal Navy was unable to stop German ships delivering and then resupplying troops, because the British warships could not operate effectively while within range of German land-based aircraft. The Royal Navy did succeed in sinking a fair number of German warships, especially

in fierce battles at Narvik. But most of Norway was in German hands by early May.

In Britain, the defeat in Norway undermined confidence in Chamberlain's leadership. On 10 May Winston Churchill replaced Chamberlain as prime minister. On Churchill's first day as prime minister, the Germans launched their long-awaited offensive on the western front.

The German army was easily outnumbered by the British and French. It even had less tanks than its opponents, though more aircraft. But the Germans

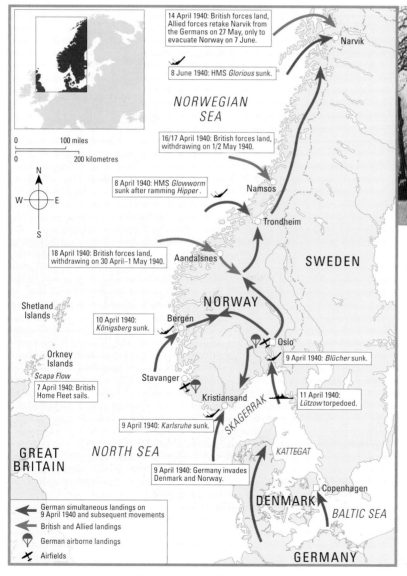

The German invasion of Norway in April 1940 was resisted by Britain and France, who also sent ships and landed troops.

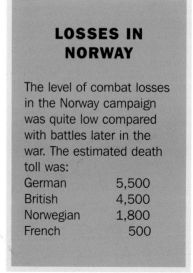

A German tank rolls unchallenged along a country road during the occupation of Denmark in April 1940. The Danes were powerless to resist the German invasion.

LOSSES IN NORWAY

The level of combat losses in the Norway campaign was quite low compared with battles later in the war. The estimated death toll was:

German	5,500
British	4,500
Norwegian	1,800
French	500

triumphed through the use of the 'Blitzkrieg' ('lightning war') tactics first employed against Poland – fast-moving armoured columns breaking through or outflanking enemy defences, with aircraft supporting the armour and causing panic and terror behind the lines.

The Germans began their offensive by invading Belgium and the Netherlands, both neutral countries. In a series of surprise attacks, German airborne troops seized bridges, airfields and the key Belgian fortress of Eben Emael, allowing armoured forces quickly to penetrate deep into enemy territory. Within five days the Dutch surrendered, but not before the port city of Rotterdam had been devastated by German bombers. Meanwhile the best elements of the British and French armies advanced into Belgium to meet the advancing Germans. This was a fatal mistake.

The Germans had originally planned to launch their main thrust through northern Belgium. But during the winter of 1939-40 Hitler had instead adopted a plan proposed by General Erich von Manstein. This called for a major attack by armoured divisions much further south, through the Ardennes region. Since the Ardennes was rough country, considered almost impassable, Allied defences in this sector were weak. Commanded by General Heinz Guderian, the spearhead of the German panzers (armoured vehicles) crossed the Meuse River near Sedan on 13 May. They broke through the Allied lines and sped north-west towards the Channel coast, which they reached on 20 May. The Allied forces in Belgium were cut off from behind.

The only option open to the hard-pressed BEF and its Allies inside Belgium was to escape by sea. Fortunately from an Allied point of view, the German armour temporarily halted its rapid advance on 23 May, leaving one Channel port still in Allied hands: Dunkirk. Between 26 May and 3 June, under constant bombardment from the air, some 338,000 men were evacuated from the port and beaches of Dunkirk. Most were carried by Royal Navy or merchant navy vessels, although a range of fishing vessels, yachts, tugs and barges crewed by civilian volunteers also played their part.

CHURCHILL DEFIANT

On 4 June 1940, Prime Minister Winston Churchill told the House of Commons: *'We shall defend our island, whatever the cost may be, we shall fight on the beaches, we shall fight on the landing grounds, we shall fight in the fields and in the streets, we shall fight in the hills; we shall never surrender.'*
[Quoted in *The Most Dangerous Enemy: A History of the Battle of Britain*, S. Bungay]

Allied troops wait to be evacuated from the beach at Dunkirk. Men formed queues into the sea, where small boats took them on board.

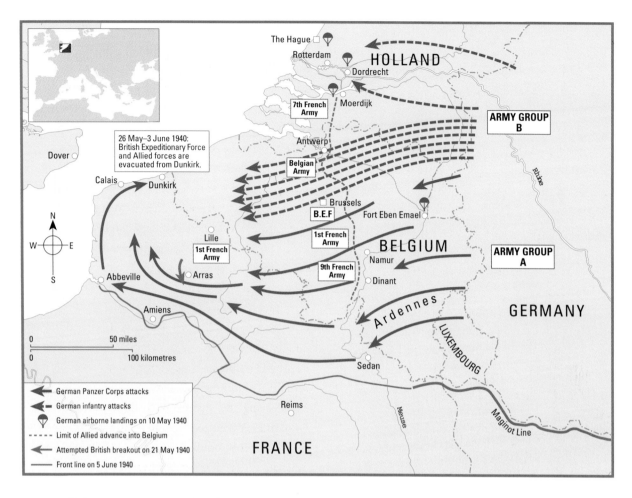

The Hague
Rotterdam
Dordrecht
HOLLAND
Moerdijk
7th French Army
Antwerp
ARMY GROUP B
Belgian Army
26 May–3 June 1940: British Expeditionary Force and Allied forces are evacuated from Dunkirk.
Dover
Calais
Dunkirk
Brussels
Fort Eben Emael
B.E.F
Lille
1st French Army
Arras
1st French Army
BELGIUM
Namur
ARMY GROUP A
9th French Army
Abbeville
Dinant
Amiens
Ardennes
GERMANY
0   50 miles
0   100 kilometres
LUXEMBOURG
Sedan
Reims
Meuse
Maginot Line
FRANCE

Rhine

German Panzer Corps attacks
German infantry attacks
German airborne landings on 10 May 1940
Limit of Allied advance into Belgium
Attempted British breakout on 21 May 1940
Front line on 5 June 1940

Dunkirk was a great escape, but the scale and speed of the German victory was still astonishing. On 5 June the Germans resumed their offensive, driving south and west into France. The French army was swept aside. On 14 June the Germans entered Paris and two days later a new French government, headed by the elderly Marshal Philippe Pétain, asked for an armistice. The fighting stopped on 25 June. The Germans occupied the north and west of France, while Pétain was left to govern the south of the country from the town of Vichy.

Although Britain had brought most of its soldiers back safely from Dunkirk, they had lost almost all their tanks, artillery and other heavy equipment. Hitler hoped that Britain, like France, would accept defeat and ask for peace terms. Some of the British government wanted to do this. But Churchill was determined to fight on. Reluctantly accepting that the British would not make peace, on 16 July Hitler ordered his generals to prepare an invasion of Britain, Operation Sealion. He also ordered an air offensive. The *Luftwaffe* –

The breakthrough of German Panzers at Sedan and their rapid progress to the Channel coast cut off the Allied armies which had advanced into Belgium further north. Dunkirk provided the only escape route from the encirclement.

German tanks advance through Belgium in May 1940. The German army's used panzer formations as a shock attack force, creating a new form of mobile warfare.

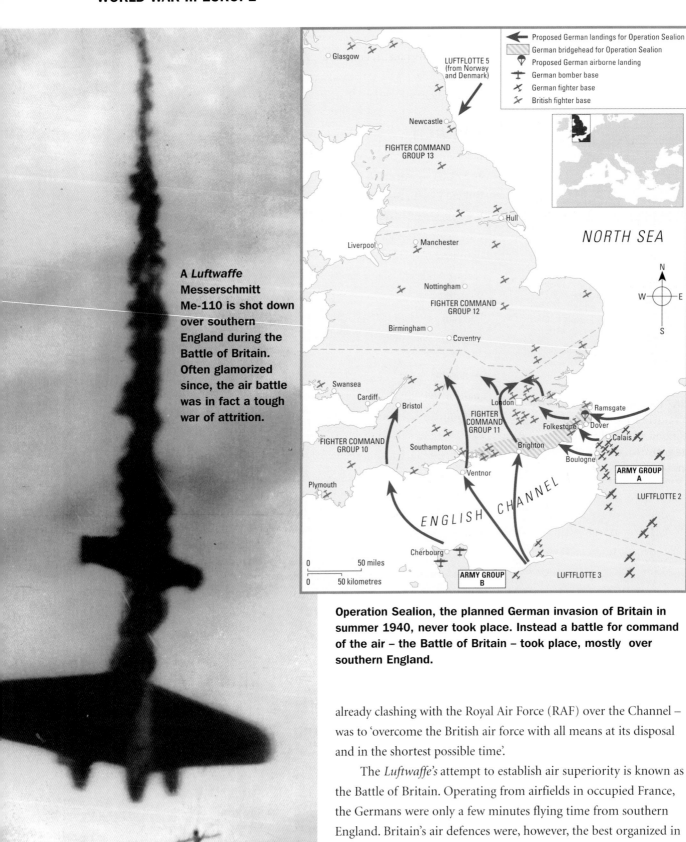

A *Luftwaffe* Messerschmitt Me-110 is shot down over southern England during the Battle of Britain. Often glamorized since, the air battle was in fact a tough war of attrition.

Legend:
- Proposed German landings for Operation Sealion
- German bridgehead for Operation Sealion
- Proposed German airborne landing
- German bomber base
- German fighter base
- British fighter base

LUFTFLOTTE 5 (from Norway and Denmark)

Glasgow
Newcastle
FIGHTER COMMAND GROUP 13
Hull
Liverpool Manchester
NORTH SEA
Nottingham
FIGHTER COMMAND GROUP 12
Birmingham
Coventry
Swansea
Cardiff
Bristol
London Ramsgate
FIGHTER COMMAND GROUP 11
Folkestone Dover
Calais
FIGHTER COMMAND GROUP 10
Southampton
Brighton
Boulogne
ARMY GROUP A
Ventnor
LUFTFLOTTE 2
Plymouth
ENGLISH CHANNEL
Cherbourg
ARMY GROUP B
LUFTFLOTTE 3

0   50 miles
0   50 kilometres

Operation Sealion, the planned German invasion of Britain in summer 1940, never took place. Instead a battle for command of the air – the Battle of Britain – took place, mostly over southern England.

already clashing with the Royal Air Force (RAF) over the Channel – was to 'overcome the British air force with all means at its disposal and in the shortest possible time'.

The *Luftwaffe's* attempt to establish air superiority is known as the Battle of Britain. Operating from airfields in occupied France, the Germans were only a few minutes flying time from southern England. Britain's air defences were, however, the best organized in the world. Radar stations and ground observers radioed warning of approaching enemy planes to operations rooms, from where orders were sent to airfields to 'scramble' the Hurricanes and Spitfires of

THE BATTLE OF BRITAIN

The *Luftwaffe's* overall losses in the Battle of Britain were far higher than the RAF's, but the RAF had more fighters downed. The *Luftwaffe* lost far more air-men because many of its aircraft shot down were bombers with a crew of four.

Luftwaffe losses:
1,887 aircraft, of which 873 were fighters; 2,698 airmen

Fighter Command losses:
1,023 aircraft; 544 airmen

RAF fighter pilots run to their aircraft to meet an attack. Every second counted, as it was vital to gain sufficient altitude before meeting the enemy.

RAF Fighter Command – flown by Canadians, New Zealanders, South Africans, Australians, Poles and Czechs as well as British pilots. Some of these fighters engaged the German Messerschmitt fighters in 'dogfights' while others took on the German bombers.

THE BLITZ From mid-August through the first week in September, the *Luftwaffe* carried out repeated attacks on airfields, aircraft factories and radar installations in an attempt to wear down resistance by the RAF. But led by Sir Hugh Dowding, Fighter Command looked after its resources well, steadily inflicting damage on the *Luftwaffe* while minimizing its own losses. On 7 September the *Luftwaffe* switched to bombing London. Mass daylight raids led to some major air battles – almost 1,000 German aircraft were involved on 15 September – but they did not bring the *Luftwaffe* any closer to achieving command of the air. By October German plans for invading Britain had been abandoned and the *Luftwaffe* was concentrating on bombing Britain's cities by night.

Dubbed 'the Blitz', the intensive night bombing campaign lasted from September 1940 to May 1941. Although London was the main target, many other cities were hit, including Liverpool, Coventry, Bristol, Plymouth, Belfast and Cardiff. At first air defences were almost powerless against night attacks and the bombers met little resistance. Only gradually did the development of radar-guided night fighters and anti-aircraft guns begin to allow the defenders to hit back. Bombing was a terrifying experience for the civilian population – some 43,000 people were killed in the Blitz. But it failed either to destroy Britain's industries or frighten the British into surrender.

It has often been said that during this period Britain 'stood alone'. But this was never altogether true. Britain had the support of her Commonwealth and also, increasingly, of the United States. When war broke out in Europe, most US citizens strongly opposed getting involved in the conflict. The spectacle of the Battle of Britain and the Blitz, however, helped to swing US opinion behind Britain. This was of great help to US President Franklin D. Roosevelt, who was personally convinced

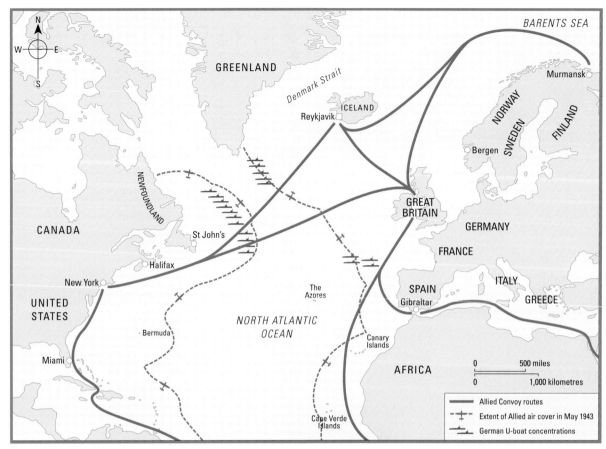

that the survival of Britain was essential to the defence of the United States.

Roosevelt at first hoped to keep the United States out of the fighting by giving Britain the tools to do the job – the USA would be 'the arsenal of democracy'. Under the Lend-Lease programme, approved by the US Congress in March 1941, the United States provided Britain with arms without immediate payment. The programme was later extended to other allies of the United States, including the Soviet Union.

The Allied supply lines across the Atlantic from the US and Canada to Britain, and north to the Soviet port of Murmansk, were crucial to Britain's survival.

President Roosevelt (left) and Prime Minister Churchill meeting on a warship in August 1941. This led to an Anglo-American declaration of principles, the Atlantic Charter.

(German submarines) which sought to cut Britain's ocean supply line. Through 1941, the United States was drawn into this conflict at sea step-by-step. By the second half of the year, without being officially at war with Germany, US naval vessels were escorting merchant convoys part way across the Atlantic.

In August 1941, Churchill and Roosevelt met on board warships off the Newfoundland coast of Canada

THE BATTLE OF THE ATLANTIC The
only way to get US-manufactured armaments and other supplies to Britain, however, was by ship. This led to the Battle of the Atlantic – a long struggle against German surface raiders and, above all, U-boats

German U-boats line up with their crews on deck.

and agreed a joint declaration of principles, the Atlantic Charter. The United States was thus already thoroughly committed to the British side in the war when Germany's Asian ally Japan attacked the US Pacific naval base at Pearl Harbor on 7 December 1941. Hitler then put an end to any further American hesitations by declaring war on the United States.

THE CODE IS BROKEN Still US

involvement in the European war would come to nothing if the Allies were unable to ferry men and equipment across the Atlantic. In 1942 U-boat 'wolf packs' sank 7.8 million tons of Allied shipping. This meant that the Allies were losing more ships than they could build. If this had continued, Britain might have had to surrender for lack of food, fuel and other essential supplies.

In 1943, however, the situation was transformed by a combination of factors, including the use of long-range aircraft on anti-submarine patrols and the cracking of German naval codes by British codebreakers. Almost 100 U-boats – a quarter of the entire German submarine force – were destroyed in the first five months of the year. They never again threatened to cut the link between the USA and Europe.

IT MUST BE DONE

In May 1941, although the United States was not yet at war with Germany, US President Franklin D. Roosevelt told the American people: *'The delivery of needed supplies to Britain is imperative. This can be done. It must be done. It will be done.'*

[Quoted in *The Second World War*, Martin Gilbert]

A depth charge explodes, watched by the crew of an Atlantic convoy escort vessel. Depth charges were used to attack submerged U-boats.

CHAPTER 3:
WAR IN THE MEDITERRANEAN

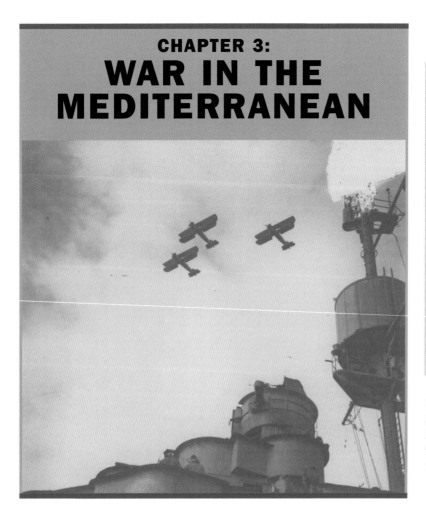

Swordfish biplanes fly over HMS *Illustrious*. Swordfish from *Illustrious* devastated the Italian fleet at Taranto in November 1940.

Despite the Axis alliance with Nazi Germany, Italian dictator Benito Mussolini did not go to war in September 1939. He was only too aware of the weaknesses of his armed forces. Instead he waited until a German victory seemed assured, declaring war on Britain and France on 10 June 1940. He hoped to exploit this opportunity to extend Italy's empire in North and East Africa and take effective control of the Mediterranean at little military cost.

Britain's position in the Mediterranean certainly looked precarious in the summer of 1940. There were British bases at Gibraltar on the southern tip of Spain, and on the island of Malta, south of Sicily. British troops were also stationed in Egypt to defend the Suez Canal, a vital communications link with the British Commonwealth, and in Palestine and Cyprus. Most of the rest of the Mediterranean was in hostile hands. Italy controlled Libya in North Africa and some of the Greek islands. Spain under General Franco was neutral but well-disposed towards Hitler and Mussolini. The French government at Vichy, which controlled southern France, collaborated with the Germans.

Britain had hopes that the French colonial authorities ruling Syria, Lebanon and French North Africa would side with General Charles de Gaulle's Free French movement, which fought alongside the British. But instead they stayed loyal to Vichy. The hostility of Vichy France to Britain was confirmed in July 1940 when the Royal Navy sank French warships in the Algerian port of Mers-el-Kebir, in order to stop them falling into the hands of the Germans.

THE ITALIANS IN AFRICA Despite the apparent weakness of Britain's position in the Mediterranean, however, it was Italy that at first suffered disaster after disaster. In North Africa, the Italian army advanced into Egypt only to be trounced by a far smaller British and Commonwealth force, which then pushed deep into

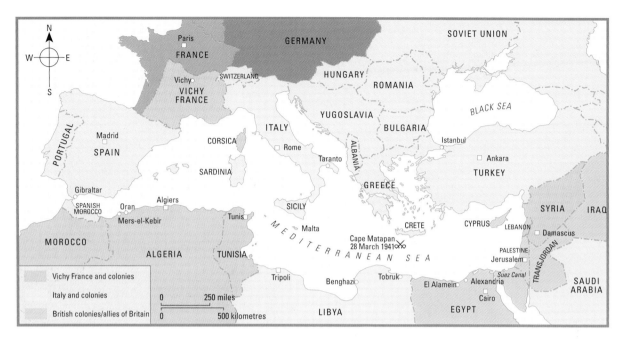

Above: In 1940, much of the Mediterranean zone was in the hands of powers hostile to Britain – Vichy France and Italy. Malta was a key staging post for the British navy between Gibraltar and Egypt.

Libya, taking 130,000 Italian prisoners. Further south, Britain evicted Italy from its recently won colony of Abyssinia, now Ethiopia. In November 1940 Swordfish biplanes from the Royal Navy aircraft carrier HMS *Illustrious* crippled three battleships and a cruiser in a daring raid on the Italian port of Taranto. The Italian navy took another battering in an encounter with the British fleet at Cape Matapan five months later. A further setback for Mussolini came in Greece, where an Italian invasion in October 1940 stalled in the face of stiff Greek resistance.

The weakness of the Italians forced the Germans to come to their aid. The arrival of German forces in the Mediterranean theatre quickly turned the situation around. *Luftwaffe* units stationed in

Italian soldiers who have surrendered to the British prepare a meal in a prisoner-of-war camp in Libya, North Africa. The Italian troops were generally poorly trained, badly led and lacking up-to-date equipment.

GERMANY

Danube

Tisza

HUNGARY

Drave
Zagreb
10 Apr 1941

Save
13 Apr 1941

ROMANIA

YUGOSLAVIA
Belgrade

Zara

Moravia

Danube

ITALY

Sarajevo

ADRIATIC SEA

Ragusa

Nitch

Skopje

Sofia

BULGARIA

Maritza

ALBANIA

Tirana

9 Apr
1941

N
W E
S

Valona

Salonika

4 May 1941

TURKEY

Mt Olympus ▲

Larissa

Lemnos

GREECE

SICILY

Lamia

AEGEAN SEA

Athens
27 April 1941
Corinth

Peloponnese
28 April 1941

Malta

MEDITERRANEAN SEA

Cape
Matapan

20 May 1941
Maleme

Heraklion

CRETE

Axis countries and their allies
Advance of Axis forces
German airborne landings
Limit of Greek advance

0   100 miles
0   200 kilometres

German parachute troops led the invasion of Crete in May 1941. The paratroopers suffered heavy losses but were able to seize a vital airfield.

Italy invaded Greece in October 1940 but the Greeks drove the invaders back into Albania. Britain sent troops to aid the Greeks, but in April 1941 the Germans quickly overran both Yugoslavia and Greece. Most of the British forces withdrew to Crete, which then also fell to Germany.

Sicily from the start of 1941 brought Malta under heavy aerial bombardment and inflicted severe punishment on British naval and merchant ships. In North Africa, German General Erwin Rommel and his Afrika Korps troops arrived in Tripoli in February 1941 and swiftly drove the British back out of Libya (see map, page 23).

One reason for Rommel's instant success was that some 60,000 British, New Zealand and Australian troops had been transferred from North Africa to Greece, in anticipation of German intervention there in support of the Italians. However, before the Germans could invade Greece, another crisis erupted in the region. In Yugoslavia, an uprising in late March 1941 overthrew the pro-German government and replaced it by a pro-British regime. Hitler immediately decided to invade Yugoslavia as well as Greece.

YUGOSLAVIA CONQUERED

Beginning on 6 April, the Germans, aided by Italian and Hungarian troops, carried out another astonishingly swift and effective campaign, routing their enemies in just three weeks. Yugoslavia was conquered and broken up, the largest single part becoming the state of Croatia, closely tied to Italy and Germany. Greece was also overrun. Some 50,000 British, Commonwealth and Greek soldiers were evacuated from southern Greece by sea, most of them being taken to the Greek island of Crete.

There followed one of the boldest military operations of the entire war. On 20 May, exploiting the fact that they had complete command of the air, the Germans launched an invasion of Crete by airborne

> ### ONE-SIDED FIGHT
> Germany's triumphs in Yugoslavia and Greece were overwhelming. The German army took prisoner: 90,000 Yugoslavs, 270,000 Greeks, 13,000 British and Commonwealth troops Germany lost some 5,000 men killed or wounded.

troops, floating down by parachute or landing in gliders. British codebreakers had provided precise information about enemy plans from intercepted messages, and German losses in the initial attack were heavy. But the Germans were allowed to seize control of an airfield at Maleme on the north of the island, after which they were able to fly in more troops and equipment in transport aircraft. By the end of the month the island was in German hands.

The British feared that the Germans might go on to capture other islands, especially Malta. But although Malta was put under siege – hammered by continual *Luftwaffe* bombing raids and almost starved into submission by the sinking of ships carrying food and fuel to the island – it was never invaded.

Once Germany had attacked the Soviet Union in June 1941 (see page 25), Hitler viewed the Mediterranean as a sideshow. Rommel had to fight on

The war in Yugoslavia was the occasion for large-scale massacres of civilians, especially Serbs killed by the Germans, Italians and Croatians.

General Bernard Montgomery was appointed commander of the British Eighth Army in North Africa in August 1942, three months before the victory at El Alamein.

THE BATTLE OF EL ALAMEIN

The forces engaged at Alamein in October-November 1942 were:

Axis

men	104,000
tanks	489
artillery	1,219
aircraft	350

Eighth Army

men	195,000
tanks	1,029
artillery	2,311
aircraft	530

British infantry advance in the desert. Such 'action' photos were almost always posed for the cameras.

in the North African desert with often inadequate resources. From the summer of 1941 to the summer of 1942, the fighting swung back and forth. Rommel generally had the better of the tank battles, but was never quite able to break through to Cairo and the Suez Canal. His last offensive was stopped at Alam Halfa, in the Egyptian desert, in August-September 1942.

The war in the desert was far more important to Britain than to the Germans because it was at the time the only place where British troops could engage the enemy in battle. The same logic dictated that the United States become involved in North Africa. In 1942 it was essential that the US Army, in the war since December 1941, should do some actual fighting against Germany and Italy. The US chiefs of staff favoured an invasion of German-occupied France, but the British persuaded them that this was too risky. The United States then opted for an invasion of French North Africa to attack Rommel's forces from the rear.

EL ALAMEIN, EGYPT On 23 October 1942 the British Eighth Army, commanded by General Bernard Montgomery, launched a large-scale offensive against a well-prepared Axis defensive line at El Alamein, Egypt. By 4 November the Eighth Army had broken through, forcing Rommel to retreat towards Tunisia. This victory was followed on 8 November by

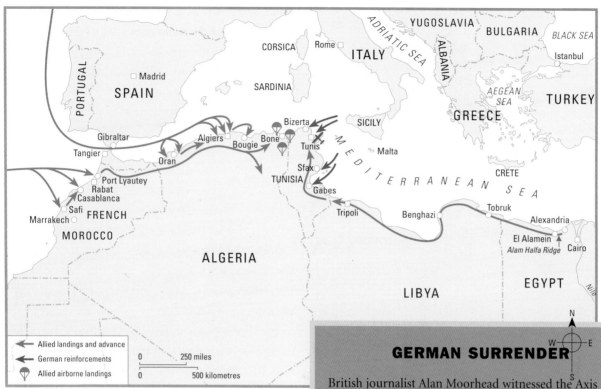

After its victory at El Alamein in October-November 1942, the British Eighth Army advanced across North Africa to Tunisia.

General Erwin Rommel was an inspired German tank commander in North Africa.

GERMAN SURRENDER

British journalist Alan Moorhead witnessed the Axis surrender in Tunisia. He wrote: *'We rode back … to Tunis, past the prisoners who now stretched in a procession reaching from the tip of Cap Bon far into Tunisia. Weeks were going to elapse before a final count revealed the total at over a quarter of a million prisoners… In all the Axis had lost close to a million men in Africa. Now they had nothing, absolutely nothing to show for it.'*

[From *African Trilogy*, Alan Moorhead]

Operation Torch, the landing in French North Africa of Allied forces commanded by General Dwight D. Eisenhower.

The last stages of the North African campaign did not go smoothly for the Allies. Unwilling to accept defeat anywhere, Hitler gave higher priority to the desert war and rushed reinforcements into Tunisia. Allied hopes that the Axis forces could be defeated by the end of 1942 were dashed. But the troops that Hitler poured into North Africa were being sacrificed in a lost cause. When the Axis forces were finally forced to surrender in May 1943, some 200,000 Germans and Italians were taken prisoner. The Allies could now use North Africa as a jumping-off point for an invasion of Italy.

CHAPTER 4:
CLASH OF GIANTS

German troops advance through the ruins of a Russian village in July 1942. The devastation of the Soviet Union by the German invaders followed Hitler's order to carry out 'a war of annihilation'.

RUTHLESS WARFARE

German army commanders accepted Hitler's view that the war with the Soviet Union would be of a different nature from the war in the west. One tank commander, General Erich Hoepner, told his men: *'This struggle has to have as its aim the smashing of present-day Russia and must consequently be carried out with unprecedented severity. Every military action must … be led by the iron will mercilessly and totally to annihilate the enemy.'*
[Quoted in *Hitler*, Vol 2., Ian Kershaw]

After the Nazi-Soviet Pact of August 1939, Soviet dictator Josef Stalin behaved as a loyal ally of Hitler, supplying Germany with food and raw materials, including oil. But as early as July 1940 Hitler informed his generals of his intention to invade the Soviet Union. Planning for the invasion, which was codenamed Operation Barbarossa, began the following December.

Hitler felt contempt and hatred for the Soviet people, both because they were communists and because they were Slavs – regarded by Hitler as an inferior sub-human race. He told his generals that they were embarking on a 'war of annihilation [total destruction]'. Victory would, Hitler believed, make Germany unbeatable, with control of vast supplies of food and raw materials. There would be no country left in Europe capable of challenging German power.

The Germans had a low opinion of the Soviet Red Army, despite its huge size, and confidently expected to achieve total victory in one to three

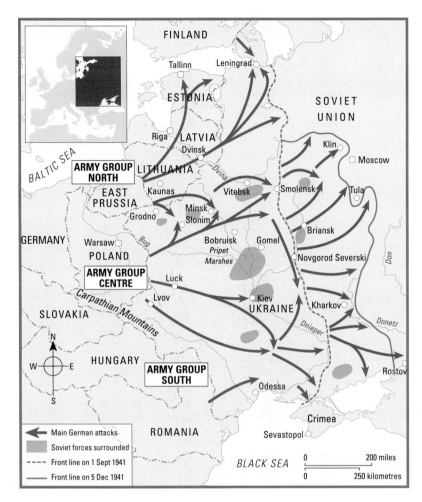

FINLAND
Tallinn
Leningrad
ESTONIA
SOVIET
UNION
Riga LATVIA
Dvinsk
Klin
Moscow
ARMY GROUP
NORTH
LITHUANIA
Dvina
EAST
PRUSSIA
Kaunas
Vitebsk
Smolensk
Tula
Minsk
Grodno
Slonim
Briansk
GERMANY
Warsaw
Bobruisk
Gomel
POLAND
Bug
Pripet
Marshes
Novgorod Severski
Don
ARMY GROUP
CENTRE
Luck
Lvov
Kiev
Kharkov
Carpathian Mountains
UKRAINE
SLOVAKIA
Dnieper
Donetz
N
W   E
S
HUNGARY
ARMY GROUP
SOUTH
Rostov
Odessa
Crimea
ROMANIA
Sevastopol

→ Main German attacks
Soviet forces surrounded
---- Front line on 1 Sept 1941
— Front line on 5 Dec 1941

BLACK SEA
0   200 miles
0   250 kilometres

Invading the Soviet Union in June 1941, German forces advanced rapidly and captured millions of Soviet soldiers. Leningrad was put under siege, but the German advance ground to a halt in December without reaching Moscow.

German soldiers found the fighting in the Soviet Union a far tougher task than earlier campaigns. They came to fear a posting to the Eastern Front as almost the same as a death sentence.

months. They intended to launch their offensive in May 1941 and win well before the dreaded Russian winter closed in. The start of Barbarossa was delayed, however, partly because of the events in Yugoslavia and Greece which required the Germans' attention in the spring (see pages 20-1). The launch of the offensive was finally set for 22 June.

For the invasion, an army over three million strong was assembled along the border with the Soviet Union, from the Baltic in the north to the Black Sea in the south. It included not only Germans but also soldiers from Romania, Hungary, Italy, Finland, Slovakia and Spain. Only a small part of this huge force consisted of armoured divisions, however, and much of the army did not even have motorized transport – there were 3,550 tanks involved in the offensive, but 700,000 horses.

Stalin received precise warnings of the coming offensive both from his own spies and from Britain, which was reading German coded messages, but failed to place his forces on full alert. As a result, the Soviet forces were taken by surprise and their shallow defensive lines were easily broken.

The Soviets had more tanks and aircraft than their enemies and Soviet soldiers fought fiercely in defence of their homeland. But they were poorly organized and poorly led. The first month of the campaign was an total disaster for them. The German Army Group Centre advanced rapidly, taking Minsk and Smolensk by mid-July (see page 25). Had they continued to advance towards Moscow, they might have taken the Soviet capital. In August, however, Hitler ordered them to turn aside to help Army Group South conquer the Ukraine. By the end of September, the encircled Soviet forces in the south had been forced to surrender at Kiev, while the German Army Group North was on the outskirts of Leningrad.

By the time the advance on Moscow resumed at the beginning of October, however, the weather was already worsening. Heavy rains were followed by snow and bitter cold. By the end of November the Germans were within 20 km of the centre of Moscow, but without clothing or equipment for a winter war, they faltered in the face of fanatical Soviet resistance. On 5 December the Soviets

counterattacked in force. Freezing cold and worn down by five months of hard fighting, for the first time in the war the Germans retreated. Moscow was saved.

THE FATE OF LENINGRAD

Unquestionably 1941 had been a catastrophic year for the Soviet armed forces. They had lost probably a million men killed and 3.5 million taken prisoner. But German losses had also been extremely heavy – around a million killed, wounded or taken captive.

The sufferings of the Soviet people were typified by the fate of Leningrad, which was kept under

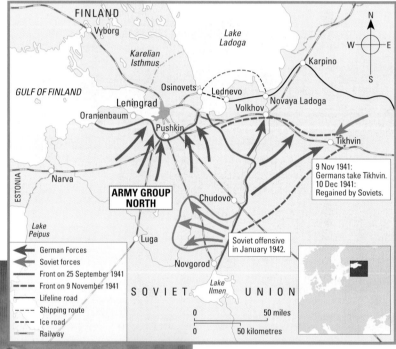

The only lifeline to besieged Leningrad was across Lake Ladoga, by boat in summer and by a road across the ice in winter.

A Soviet propaganda photograph shows snipers in snow camouflage fighting on the Leningrad front in 1943. Soviet troops generally coped better with fighting in severe winter weather conditions than their German enemy.

Cossack cavalry, from the Don region of the Soviet Union, ride out on patrol. Despite the use of tanks and trucks, horses played an important role in warfare on the Eastern Front.

OVERWHELMED BY DEATH

A Leningrad resident, Vera Inber, writing in her diary in December 1941, described how people were overwhelmed by the scale of the deaths in the besieged city: '*The mortuary itself is full. Not only are there too few trucks to go to the cemetery, but, more important, no gasoline to put in the trucks and the main thing is – there is not enough strength left in the living to bury the dead.*'

[Quoted in *Russia's War*, Richard Overy]

blockade by the Germans for 900 days from September 1941 to February 1944. The city's only lifeline to the outside world was across Lake Ladoga – by boat in summer and over the ice in winter. Around a million of the Leningrad population died either under bombardment or of starvation and disease. The terrible brutality of German rule in the occupied areas ensured that, even among people who had suffered injustice and oppression under Stalin, there were very few inclined to collaborate with the invaders.

German artillery shells a factory in Stalingrad in 1942. Named after the Soviet dictator, the city became a prize neither side felt they could afford to lose.

The survival of the Soviet Union came as a huge relief to Britain and the United States, who desperately needed Stalin as an ally against Hitler. Stalin equally need the Western Allies, who provided a generous flow of modern military equipment, delivered to the Red Army via the Arctic port of Murmansk. But in factories relocated to safety beyond the Ural mountains, the Soviets were also soon producing their own armaments in vast quantities, including tanks and aircraft that were a match for anything the Germans had.

In 1942, however, it still looked as if Hitler might win the war in the Soviet Union. In the first half of the year the Soviets exhausted their strength in a series of costly and largely unsuccessful counterattacks. The Germans then launched a devastating offensive in the south that carried them to the Caucasus mountains, threatening the vital Baku oilfields. At the same time, the German Sixth Army advanced on Stalingrad, a city on the Volga river.

The Germans reached the suburbs of Stalingrad in mid-September, but the Soviets defended the city building by building and street by street. Two months later, elements of the Red Army were still holding out in the city with their backs to the river. Then, on 19 November, Soviet forces counterattacked north and south of Stalingrad. They formed a noose around the city, with the German Sixth Army trapped inside. All efforts to break the iron ring around Stalingrad failed. Despite an impressive effort to supply the Sixth Army by air in terrible weather conditions, the German troops ran short of food and ammunition. On 31 January 1943 German Sixth Army commander Field Marshal Friedrich Paulus finally surrendered.

Stalingrad was a crushing defeat for Hitler and marked the turning point of the war. The Germans had reached the limits of their power. From then onwards, the forces ranged against Hitler would only get stronger, as the Soviet Union and the United States brought their vast reserves of manpower and industrial productivity to bear on the war.

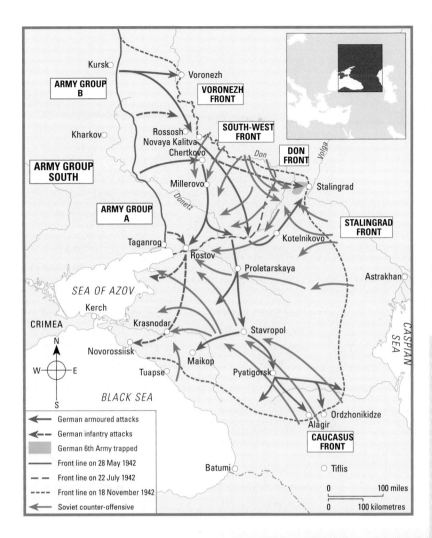

ARMY GROUP B

VORONEZH FRONT

SOUTH-WEST FRONT

DON FRONT

ARMY GROUP SOUTH

ARMY GROUP A

STALINGRAD FRONT

CAUCASUS FRONT

Kursk

Voronezh

Kharkov

Rossosh
Novaya Kalitva
Chertkovo

Don

Volga

Millerovo

Stalingrad

Donetz

Taganrog

Rostov

Kotelnikovo

Proletarskaya

Astrakhan

SEA OF AZOV

Kerch

CRIMEA

Krasnodar

Stavropol

CASPIAN SEA

N
W E
S

Novorossiisk

Maikop

Pyatigorsk

Tuapse

Ordzhonikidze

Alagir

BLACK SEA

Batumi

Tiflis

	German armoured attacks
	German infantry attacks
	German 6th Army trapped
	Front line on 28 May 1942
	Front line on 22 July 1942
	Front line on 18 November 1942
	Soviet counter-offensive

0   100 miles
0   100 kilometres

In the summer of 1942 the Germans advanced to Stalingrad and towards the oilfields in the Caucasus. The Soviet counter-offensive in November cut off the German army in Stalingrad.

Below: Some of the 91,000 German soldiers taken prisoner by the Soviets in the battle of Stalingrad: most would die in captivity.

LOSSES AT STALINGRAD

Although Stalingrad was a defeat for the Germans, it is generally accepted that Soviet casualties were heavier. They could afford such losses; the Germans could not. The majority of the German prisoners taken at Stalingrad died in captivity.
German losses: 147,000 dead, 91,000 prisoners
Soviet losses: c.500,000

CHAPTER 5: OCCUPIED EUROPE

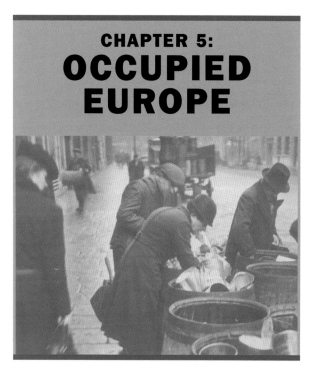

At the peak of its success in the war, Nazi Germany controlled a vast area of Europe from the Atlantic to the Caucasus and from Norway to the Mediterranean. Every country on the European mainland except the Soviet Union had either been conquered, or was allied with Germany, or was a neutral that made itself useful to the Nazis.

Throughout German-occupied Europe there were shortages of food and other life essentials. Here French people search through refuse in the hope of finding scraps to eat.

At the end of 1942, German domination of Europe was at its fullest extent. The Wehrmacht had recently occupied Vichy France and pushed deep inside the Soviet Union.

- Greater German Reich
- Countries administered by Germany
- Territory accupied by the Wehrmacht
- Allies of Germany and satellite countries

NORWAY · FINLAND · SWEDEN · ESTONIA · LATVIA · LITHUANIA · SOVIET UNION · NORTH SEA · IRELAND · DENMARK · BALTIC SEA · WHITE RUSSIA · GREAT BRITAIN · NETHERLANDS · BELGIUM · GERMANY · POLISH GENERAL GOVERNMENT · UKRAINE · ATLANTIC OCEAN · SLOVAKIA · FRANCE · SWITZERLAND · HUNGARY · ROMANIA · CROATIA · SERBIA · BLACK SEA · PORTUGAL · SPAIN · CORSICA · ITALY · MONTENEGRO · ALBANIA · BULGARIA · SARDINIA · TURKEY · MEDITERRANEAN SEA · SICILY · GREECE · MOROCCO · CRETE · CYPRUS · SYRIA · LEBANON · IRAQ · ALGERIA · TUNISIA · PALESTINE · TRANSJORDAN · LIBYA · EGYPT · SAUDI ARABIA

0 — 250 miles
0 — 500 kilometres

MASTER RACE

Many Poles were deported to Germany for use as slave labour. Instructions issued by the Nazis to Germans who found themselves working alongside Poles stressed German racial superiority: *'Germans, the Pole is never your friend. He is inferior to every German on your farm or in your factory. Remember that you belong to the master nation.'*
[Quoted in *The Second World War*, Henri Michel]

A French Resistance fighter is prepared for execution by a German firing squad. The Germans on many occasions executed groups of prisoners in retaliation for the killing of German officers or soldiers by the Resistance.

In most countries that the Nazis occupied (Poland was one exception) they found political movements that were keen to imitate Nazi policies and that collaborated enthusiastically with the occupiers. The Vichy French government of Marshal Pétain, for example, actively collaborated with the Nazis even before the area of France it governed was occupied by German troops, which did not happen until the end of 1942. Collaborators were often known as 'Quislings', after the Norwegian Nazi leader Vidkun Quisling, head of government in Occupied Norway.

STARVATION AND NEGLECT
The scale of suffering under Nazi rule was almost unimaginable. Within Nazi-occupied Europe, many millions of people died in the course of the war – systematically or casually slaughtered by the Germans and their allies, or allowed to die of starvation or neglect.

The immediate demands of the war effort led the Germans to exploit conquered territories ever more intensely as the war became more desperate. For conquered peoples, this led to hardship and malnutrition. A growing labour shortage in Germany was met by forcibly importing hundreds of thousands of foreign workers, or using prisoners of war and inmates of concentration camps as slaves who were forced to work in factories and on building projects.

But the way the Nazis behaved was also based on their long-term aim to create a 'New Order' on the continent. The Nazi New Order was to be a Europe based on the domination of the so-called Aryan race – Germans and other blond, blue-eyed people – over the rest. The Slavs, regarded as sub-human, were to be either reduced to slavery or exterminated to make room for German settlers in the east. The Poles (a Slav people) lost about one in five of their population in the course of the war. Soviet prisoners of war (also Slavs) died in their millions in German camps, and further millions of Soviet citizens perished during the occupation. The Roma and Sinti (Gypsy) people of Europe also suffered grievously under Nazi rule.

THE JEWS

The only people worse treated than the Slavs were the Jews. German military successes brought around eight million Jewish people under Nazi rule. There was no room for them in the Nazi New Order. Europe was to be 'cleansed' of Jews, strangely regarded by Hitler as a demonic race responsible for Germany's and the world's ills. From 1941 onwards, the Nazis embarked upon a 'Final Solution' of the 'Jewish problem'. They set out systematically to exterminate the Jewish people – men, women and children. At first, hundreds of thousands were killed by firing squad or gassed in the back of vans. Then death camps were established at sites inside occupied Poland – Majdanek, Chelmno, Treblinka, Sobibor, Belzec, Auschwitz – where Jews were killed in purpose-built gas chambers. The Nazis devoted massive resources to organizing the transportation of Jews from all over Europe to the death camps. It is estimated that about six million Jews were killed in the Holocaust.

The brutality of Nazi rule inevitably led to resistance. Secret movements were set up in all occupied countries. Their activities ranged from organizing acts of passive resistance such as strikes or the concealment of Jews from their persecutors, to sabotage, assassinations, uprisings and full-scale guerrilla warfare. The largest armed resistance movements were in the occupied areas of the Soviet Union and in Yugoslavia, where two mutually hostile guerrilla armies, one led by the communist Josip Broz Tito and the other by the Royalist Colonel Draza Mihailovic, fought the Germans, Italians and Croats. Other substantial partisan groups included those in the south of France and in northern Italy towards the end of the war.

Resistance movements pinned down considerable numbers of German troops which could have been used elsewhere in the war. In Poland, for example, when the underground Home Army staged an armed insurrection in Warsaw in 1944, more than 20,000

These ovens at the Dachau concentration camp in Germany were used to cremate the bodies of prisoners killed by the Nazis.

Jewish people deported to Auschwitz by the Germans wait to discover their fate. Many, including almost all children, were gassed to death within hours of arrival at Auschwitz.

German troops, backed by airpower, were engaged for two months in putting down the uprising. But resistance groups were never strong enough to drive out the occupation forces unaided.

Britain tried to encourage resistance through the Special Operations Executive (SOE), set up in 1940, later helped by the American Office of Strategic Services (OSS). The SOE and OSS sent secret agents into Occupied Europe, as well as delivering arms and equipment to resistance groups. These perilous operations cost many brave people their lives but had limited effect.

As well as encouraging resistance movements, between

The Nazi camps dedicated to the extermination of Jews were situated in the Polish General Government – German-occupied Poland. Concentration camps, used mostly to provide slave labour, were mainly in Germany. Auschwitz was both a concentration camp and an extermination camp.

SAVED BY SLAVERY

The lives of many Jews and Slavs were saved by the German need for slave labour in their factories, which led the Nazis reluctantly to keep them alive. Hitler's propaganda chief Joseph Goebbels wrote in his diary in March 1941: *'We have to go easy on the 30,000 Jews who work in armaments production; we need them – who would have thought this could ever become possible?'*

[Quoted in *The Holocaust*, R.G. Grant]

A German soldier supervises the burial of massacred Polish Jews, probably in late 1941. The men digging would then also be killed.

1940 and 1943 the Western Allies carried out a few scattered coastal raids on German-occupied Europe. The largest of these, a landing at Dieppe, northern France, by Canadian troops in August 1942, was a disaster, with over 3,000 of the 5,000 troops involved either killed or taken prisoner.

THE BOMBING OFFENSIVE

There was one way, however, in which the Allies could strike at the very heart of Germany. This was through air attack. From 1940 onwards RAF Bomber Command carried out raids on Germany and in 1942 the

The scene in Hamburg after the devastation of the city by bombing in 1943. American bombers attacked Germany by day and the RAF did the same by night.

US daylight bombing raids were at first launched from East Anglia in Britain. From 1943 onwards, bases in North Africa and Italy brought targets such as the Ploesti oilfields in Romania within range.

PROFIT AND LOSS

The effectiveness of the Allied bombing campaign has been much disputed. Huge resources were devoted to it – the RAF alone dropped almost a million tons of bombs on Germany. The RAF and USAAF also paid a heavy price in lost lives. Yet, as well as the damage it caused, the bombing offensive forced the Germans to devote major resources to homeland defence – it occupied the cream of their air force. The death toll among bomber crews and civilians was:
RAF Bomber Command aircrew 55,500 killed
USAAF Eighth Air Force aircrew 26,000 killed
German civilians killed 600,000

American B-24 Liberator bombers turn for home after raiding a German airfield.

US Army Air Force (USAAF) joined in the bombing campaign. Based in eastern England, the USAAF carried out its bombing raids by day, depending on the firepower of its high-flying bombers to hold off German fighter aircraft. The RAF bombed by night, relying on the cover of darkness to get through the enemy defences.

The bombing offensive was on a massive scale. In mid-1942 the RAF carried out raids with over a thousand bombers in the sky at the same time. The night raids were often inaccurate and the bombers suffered heavy losses, but they could have a devastating effect on cities. In one night in July 1943, an RAF raid on Hamburg is reckoned to have killed over 40,000 German civilians. Bombing by day, the Americans sought to be more accurate, aiming to hit specific factories or other economic or military targets. Bad weather and the intensity of German anti-aircraft defences meant, however, that the US bombers also often missed their targets and paid a high price. In

August 1943, for example, the USAAF lost 60 bombers in a single day.

As the war went on, Allied bombing became increasingly effective. Allied advances in the Mediterranean meant that bombers were able to operate from North Africa and Italy as well as England. The introduction of the P-51 Mustang long-range fighter as a bomber escort in 1944 at last gave day bombers a real defence against German fighters. Improvements in navigation and tactics made even night bombers reasonably accurate. Although German factories never ceased to function, the bombing of sources of fuel supplies, especially the Ploesti oilfields in Romania, had a crippling effect on the German war machine in the last year of the war.

There was no let up in the air offensive as the war drew to a close. The Allied bombing of the city of Dresden in February 1945 may have killed over 50,000 people. By then most German cities, including the capital Berlin, had been reduced to ruins.

CHAPTER 6:
THE TIDE TURNS

British troops wade ashore during the Allied invasion of Sicily in July 1943. This was the start of long hard fight up the Italian peninsula which continued for the rest of the war.

MONASTERY DESTROYED

One of the most controversial decisions of the war was made by Allied commanders in February 1944 when they ordered the bombing of the 1400-year-old monastery of Monte Cassino. Commenting on the decision, General Eisenhower said: *'If we have to choose between destroying a famous building and sacrificing our own men, then our men's lives count infinitely more, and the buildings must go.'*

[Quoted on the Texas Military Forces Museum website]

By 1943 Britain and the United States were keen to invade mainland Europe to create a 'Second Front' that would bring relief to the Soviet Union, which was doing the bulk of the fighting against Germany. At a meeting held in Casablanca, Morocco, in January of that year, Roosevelt and Churchill chose Sicily as the target for their troops to re-enter Europe – a much easier option than attempting landings on the north coast of Occupied France.

North Africa was cleared of Axis forces in May 1943 (see page 23). The following July Allied troops – American and British Commonwealth in almost equal numbers – crossed the Mediterranean. With supremacy both in the air and at sea, the Allies carried off the landings fairly smoothly, but they had to overcome some stubborn resistance from German forces on the island. Sicily was in Allied hands by mid-August.

The invasion of Sicily was the final blow to the prestige of Italian dictator Benito Mussolini. He was deposed and replaced by an Italian army officer, Marshal Pietro Badoglio. Although Badoglio assured the Germans that Italy would carry on fighting, he secretly sought peace with the Allies. An armistice between Italy and the Allies was announced in early September, while the Allies invaded mainland Italy across the Straits of Messina from Sicily and by landing on the beaches at Salerno.

But the Germans, commanded by Field Marshal Albert Kesselring, were swift to disarm Italian troops and take over the defence of the Italian peninsula. The Salerno landings were fiercely resisted by German Panzers. Eventually forced to withdraw, the Germans pulled back in good order and stood firm along the Gustav Line, centred on the famous monastery of Monte Cassino. The advance of the Allied army – a multinational force including, among others, Poles, Indians, New Zealanders and French North African troops – ground to a halt. Cassino did not fall until mid-May, three months after the bombing of the monastery (see box above), after a lot more hard fighting to clear the Allied advance.

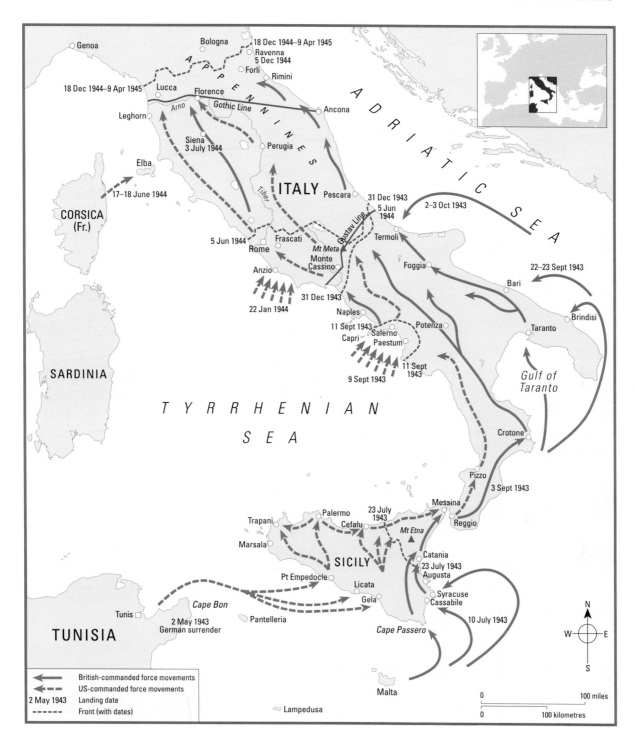

THE 'SOFT UNDERBELLY OF EUROPE'

In an attempt to get the advance moving again, in January 1944 the Allies landed a force at Anzio, between the Gustav Line and Rome, but the Germans reacted swiftly and hemmed in the landing force. The Allies did not enter Rome until the following June – and they still faced a further series of German defensive lines to the north. Once optimistically described by Churchill as the 'soft underbelly of Europe', Italy had proved to be nothing of the sort.

The Allied occupation of Sicily and then the invasion of mainland Italy in September 1943 brought hopes of swift progress. But the advance stalled in front of Cassino, and despite the Anzio landings in January 1944, two years of fighting were needed to reach northern Italy.

Soviet Katyusha multiple rocket launchers – popularly known as 'Stalin's Organs' – prepare to fire during the Soviet counter-offensive against the German invaders. Fired in volleys, the rockets could deliver a devastating artillery barrage.

Soviet troops advance through a Polish city in 1944. Around one fifth of the Polish population died during the war, either killed in the fighting or massacred by one side or the other.

Although the fighting in Italy was fierce, it was dwarfed by the scale and savagery of the conflict on the eastern front. There the Soviet offensive of the winter of 1942-3, which had brought victory at Stalingrad, had carried the Red Army forwards to a line that pushed out west of the city of Kursk. In July 1943, the Germans launched an armoured counterattack against the Kursk salient, hoping for a crushing victory that would once more give them the upper hand. But for the first time the German armour and its air support had met their match. In the largest armoured battle ever seen, with more than 2,000 tanks committed on each side, the German offensive was repulsed and a Soviet counterattack forced the Germans to retreat.

BACK TOWARDS GERMANY From that point onwards, the tide of war on the eastern front flowed in only one direction – back towards Germany. The Soviets now had tanks and aircraft as good as, or better than, those of the Germans, and their commanders used them with flair and intelligence. In September 1943 the Red Army reached the Dniepr River, and the following November they took the Ukrainian capital, Kiev. Soviet casualties were consistently much higher than those suffered by the Germans, but the Germans were increasingly outnumbered. About three million Axis troops faced over six million Soviet soldiers at the end of 1943, and the Soviets had a similar superiority of numbers in tanks and aircraft.

The siege of Leningrad was lifted in February 1944 and by May most of the Ukraine and Crimea were back in Soviet hands. The greatest remaining obstacle to the Red Army's advance was German Army Group Centre, which continued to occupy Belorussia. In June 1944 the Soviets

After the victory at Kursk in the summer of 1943, the Soviet Red Army drove the Germans out of the Soviet Union. In the centre their advance came to a halt just short of Warsaw.

launched Operation Bagration, a vast and complex offensive that in five weeks drove Army Group Centre hundreds of kilometres back across the pre-war Soviet border into Poland.

At the end of July the Red Army's advance in Poland stopped on the east bank of the Vistula, the river that runs through the Polish capital, Warsaw. The Soviets took no action to help the Polish Home

Army's uprising in the city (see pages 32-3), which was put down by the Germans with such ferocity that over 200,000 Polish civilians were killed. The Soviet advance continued further south, however. In the second half of 1944 Soviet forces entered Romania, Hungary and Yugoslavia, reaching the outskirts of the Hungarian capital, Budapest, by the end of the year.

WORLD WAR II: EUROPE

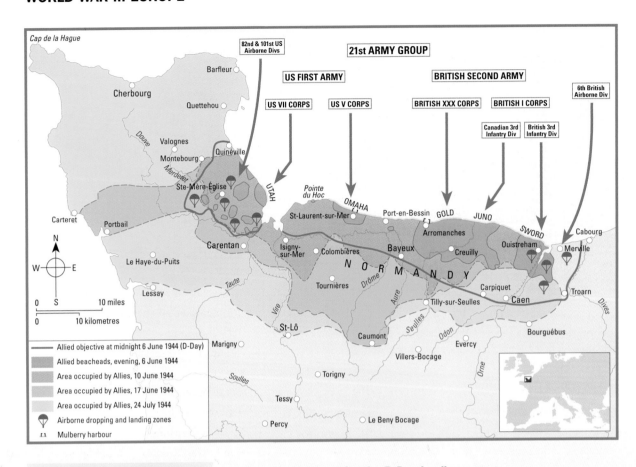

Cap de la Hague

Barfleur

Cherbourg

Quettehou

82nd & 101st US Airborne Divs

21st ARMY GROUP

US FIRST ARMY

BRITISH SECOND ARMY

6th British Airborne Div

US VII CORPS

US V CORPS

BRITISH XXX CORPS

BRITISH I CORPS

Canadian 3rd Infantry Div

British 3rd Infantry Div

Douve

Valognes

Montebourg

Quinéville

Merderet

Ste-Mère-Église

UTAH

Pointe du Hoc

OMAHA

St-Laurent-sur-Mer

Port-en-Bessin

GOLD

JUNO

SWORD

Cabourg

Carteret

Portbail

Carentan

Isigny-sur-Mer

Colombières

Bayeux

Arromanches

Creuilly

Ouistreham

Merville

Le Haye-du-Puits

Taute

Vire

Tournières

Drôme

N O R M A N D Y

Aure

Carpiquet

Caen

Troarn

Dives

Lessay

Tilly-sur-Seulles

Seulles

Odon

Bourguébus

St-Lô

Marigny

Soulles

Caumont

Villers-Bocage

Evercy

Orne

Torigny

Tessy

Percy

Le Beny Bocage

N / W E / S

0 ——— 10 miles
0 ——— 10 kilometres

— Allied objective at midnight 6 June 1944 (D-Day)
■ Allied beacheads, evening, 6 June 1944
■ Area occupied by Allies, 10 June 1944
■ Area occupied by Allies, 17 June 1944
■ Area occupied by Allies, 24 July 1944
⚐ Airborne dropping and landing zones
⌂ Mulberry harbour

D-DAY LANDINGS

Landing over 130,000 men on fortified beaches, the Allies expected heavier casualties on D-Day, 6 June 1944, than they actually suffered:

Troops landed
75,215 British and Canadian
57,500 American

Casualties
4,300 British and Canadian
6,000 American

The beaches chosen for the D-Day landings were code-named Utah, Omaha, Gold, Juno and Sword.

American troops wade ashore on Omaha beach during the Normandy landings.

Allied Supreme Commander Dwight Eisenhower talking to men of the US 101st Airborne Division in advance of the D-Day Normandy landings.

The desperate situation of the Germans on the eastern front was matched by the situation in the west. On 6 June 1944 – known as D-Day – the Western Allies began the long-awaited invasion of France with landings on the coast of Normandy. Carefully planned under the direction of Allied Supreme Commander General Dwight Eisenhower, Operation Overlord was the largest seaborne invasion ever launched, involving 1,200 warships, 5,000 landing craft and troop transports, and 10,000 aircraft. Two artificial harbours ('Mulberries') were towed across the Channel, so the army could be supplied and reinforced once ashore.

UTAH, OMAHA, GOLD, JUNO AND SWORD
All the careful preparation was almost undone by the weather, which was so rough it seemed the invasion would have to be abandoned. Gambling on a brief break in the storms predicted by weather forecasters, however, Eisenhower embarked his US, British and Canadian troops in southern England for a night-time crossing to France. Airborne troops were dropped into Normandy under cover of darkness, and at dawn the seaborne troops landed on five beaches – codenamed Utah, Omaha, Gold, Juno and Sword.

The invaders had some key advantages. Their command of the air and the sea was such that the German air force and navy barely interfered. A clever deception plan had convinced Hitler that the invasion would come in the area around Calais (a port about 250 km north-east along the coast), so that even when news of the landings came through, he remained convinced that it was only a diversionary attack. The destruction of communications links by Allied bombers in any case made it hard for the Germans to move reinforcements swiftly to Normandy.

Yet the success of the landings was a close-run affair. The coast was heavily fortified. On Omaha beach, the American 1st Infantry Division suffered heavy casualties and was very nearly driven back into the sea. When a beachhead was established, progress was still slow. Montgomery's British and Canadian troops took over a month to capture Caen, a town they had hoped to occupy on the first day of the invasion. The weather remained a problem, with low cloud blocking air operations and storms wrecking one of the Mulberry harbours in the third week of June. The capture of the port of Cherbourg at the end of the month was a step forwards, but the failure to break through encircling German defences meant that

A French woman takes a close look at a knocked out German tank in a Normandy town. The German panzers fought skilfully and tenaciously, but they were vulnerable to Allied air attack.

US paratroopers advance as shells explode around them during Operation Market Garden in 1944.

growing numbers of Allied troops and quantities of supplies were bottled up in north-west Normandy.

In late July, while Canadian and British forces engaged the bulk of the German armoured divisions, US forces at last made the long-awaited breakout from Normandy, fanning out from Avranches west into Brittany and east towards the River Seine. The Germans launched a counterattack against Avranches, but suffered heavy losses and were threatened with encirclement as Canadian troops from the north prepared to link up with Americans swinging up from the south near the town of Falaise. Many of the Germans managed to escape eastwards before the 'Falaise Gap' was closed on 20 August, but nothing could now stop the Allies' rapid progress. On the same day, the spearhead of the US forces crossed the Seine.

On 15 August a new front had been opened by Allied landings in Provence on France's Mediterranean coast. The French Resistance was in open armed revolt, taking on the German army in many parts of France, including Paris. A Free French armoured division was allowed the honour of liberating the city on 25 August, preparing the way for Free French leader General Charles de Gaulle to form a new government to replace the discredited Vichy regime.

SUMMER 1944 In the heady days of summer 1944 it was easy to imagine that the war in Europe would be over by the end of the year. Two million Allied troops, 60 per cent of them from the USA, were advancing on Germany from the west while the largest part of the German army was still forced to remain facing the Soviets in the east. Montgomery's British Second Army liberated the Belgian capital, Brussels, in the first week of September, by which time General George Patton's US Third Army had reached the Moselle River, only 160 km from the Rhine.

At this point, though, the Allies lost momentum. In Belgium, they captured the major port of Antwerp intact, with the help of the Belgian Resistance, but were unable to use it immediately because the

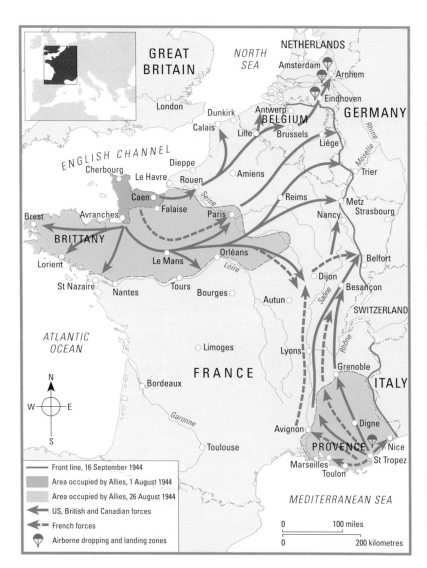

The liberation of France was achieved in August-September 1944, but the attempted breakthrough into Germany via Arnhem was a failure.

GERMAN WEAKNESS

It has often been debated whether a more vigorous offensive strategy could have allowed Allied troops to break through into Germany in the autumn of 1944. A German officer, General Westphal, wrote after the war: '*The overall situation in the West was serious in the extreme… Until the middle of October [1944] the enemy could have broken through at any point he liked with ease, and would have then been able to cross the Rhine and thrust deep into Germany almost unhindered.*'

[Quoted in *History of the Second World War*, B. H. Liddel Hart]

Germans remained in control of the River Scheldt leading into the port. It became increasingly difficult to keep the Allied armies supplied via now distant Normandy ports, and the advance ground to a halt.

In a bold attempt to end the war quickly, on 17 September Montgomery launched Operation Market Garden. Some 20,000 Allied airborne troops were dropped into the Occupied Netherlands by parachute and glider. They were to seize and hold a series of key bridges, allowing Allied tanks to drive across the Netherlands and into the Ruhr, Germany's industrial heartland. But the final river crossing, at Arnhem, proved 'a bridge too far'. British paratroops could not hold it and the armoured column failed to reach it in time. This failure condemned the Allies to continue fighting through the winter into 1945.

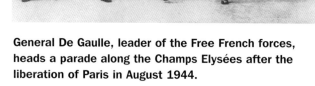

General De Gaulle, leader of the Free French forces, heads a parade along the Champs Elysées after the liberation of Paris in August 1944.

CHAPTER 7

THE ROAD TO BERLIN

American tanks struggle to cope with the weather conditions in northern France during the Battle of the Bulge in the winter of 1944-5.

By the summer of 1944 many senior German army officers were desperate to end the war before it resulted in the total destruction of their country. They led a plot to assassinate Hitler, overthrow the Nazi regime and sue for peace. On 20 July 1944 the conspirators planted a time bomb at Hitler's headquarters in East Prussia. But although the explosion injured the dictator, he survived. Almost all those who had plotted against him were arrested and cruelly executed.

It was far from certain that a non-Nazi German regime could have negotiated a peace deal, since the Allies had adopted a policy of 'unconditional surrender' – meaning that the Germans must simply accept defeat and allow the victors to do with them what they pleased. It was certain, though, that with Hitler alive peace was out of the question. Hitler would never agree to surrender, so the total conquest of Germany was the only sure path to end the war.

Faced with an apparently hopeless situation, Hitler put his faith in German 'secret weapons' which entered the war in 1944. One of these, the first jet aircraft, had only a marginal effect on the conflict. Of more impact

FAITH IN VICTORY

Hitler's generals felt that the December 1944 Ardennes offensive was absurdly over-ambitious. According to Field Marshal Gerd von Rundstedt, ordinary German soldiers did not share this scepticism: *'The morale of the troops taking part was astonishingly high at the start of the offensive. They really believed victory was possible – unlike the higher command-ers, who knew the facts.'*

[Quoted in *History of the Second World War*, B. H. Liddel Hart]

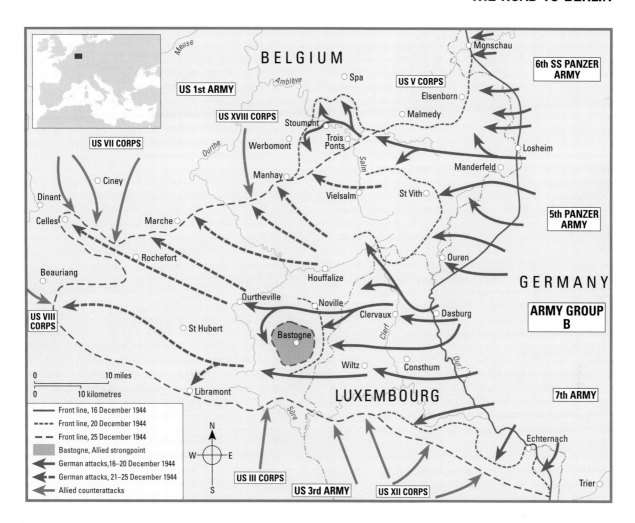

Map labels:
BELGIUM
GERMANY
LUXEMBOURG

US 1st ARMY
US XVIII CORPS
US VII CORPS
US V CORPS
US VIII CORPS
US III CORPS
US 3rd ARMY
US XII CORPS

6th SS PANZER ARMY
5th PANZER ARMY
ARMY GROUP B
7th ARMY

Monschau
Spa
Elsenborn
Malmedy
Losheim
Stoumont
Trois Ponts
Manderfeld
Werbomont
Manhay
Vielsalm
St Vith
Ciney
Dinant
Celles
Marche
Rochefort
Ouren
Beauriang
Houffalize
Ourtheville
Noville
Clervaux
Dasburg
St Hubert
Bastogne
Wiltz
Consthum
Libramont
Echternach
Trier

Rivers: Meuse, Amblève, Ourthe, Salm, Clerf, Our, Sûre

0   10 miles
0   10 kilometres

Front line, 16 December 1944
Front line, 20 December 1944
Front line, 25 December 1944
Bastogne, Allied strongpoint
German attacks, 16–20 December 1944
German attacks, 21–25 December 1944
Allied counterattacks

N W E S

were the 'V weapons'. The V-1 was a pilotless aircraft packed with explosives. The V-2 was the world's first supersonic ballistic missile – the forerunner of all today's space rockets. Fired chiefly at London and Antwerp, the V-1s and V-2s did a lot of damage. Together they killed almost 9,000 people in England. But they fell far short of having a decisive effect – for that they would have needed a nuclear warhead.

ARMOURED OFFENSIVE – BATTLE OF THE BULGE
Let down by his secret weapons, in December 1944 Hitler decided to gamble on a shock German counterattack. In virtually a repeat of May 1940, he ordered an armoured offensive through the Ardennes region of Belgium. The tanks were to break through the Allied lines and advance rapidly across the River Meuse to the coast, taking the vital port of Antwerp.

Launched on 16 December, the Ardennes offensive (popularly known as the Battle of the Bulge) at first had just the success Hitler must have hoped for. The Ardennes front was thinly held by American forces and

The German offensive of winter 1944 is known as the Battle of the Bulge because of the way it pushed into Allied-held territory.

A V-1 pilotless aircraft photographed over Britain in 1945. The V-1 would dive when its fuel ran out, exploding on contact with the ground.

surprise was complete. Allied aircraft, which could have countered the German advance, were grounded by severe winter weather.

The Americans, however, reacted swiftly. Reinforcements were rushed in, tripling the US forces in the Ardennes within four days. American soldiers, especially those encircled at Bastogne, fought with great bravery. The German forces never reached the Meuse. On 23 December the weather lifted and Allied aircraft struck against the exposed enemy forces. On 26 December Patton's armour, on the advance from Normandy, relieved Bastogne (see page 45). By then German tanks and aircraft were running out of fuel. Through January 1945, in deep snow, the Germans made a fighting withdrawal back into their homeland. They had suffered around 100,000 casualties, as well as losing hundreds of aircraft and most of their tanks. Hitler had made his last gamble and lost.

The only hope left to the German dictator was that the Western Allies and the Soviet Union would fall out.

NOBLE CRUSADE

The Allied advance revealed to the outside world the full horror of the Nazi death camps and concentration camps. For most people, this removed any doubts about whether the war was justified. British historian A.J.P. Taylor, who lived through World War II, wrote: '*No English soldier who rode with the tanks into liberated Belgium or saw the German murder camps at Dachau or Buchenwald could doubt that the war had been a noble crusade.*'

[From *English History 1914-1945*, A.J.P. Taylor]

But in February 1945 Roosevelt, Churchill and Stalin, meeting at the Ukrainian port of Yalta in the Crimea (see page 25), reached broad agreement on the

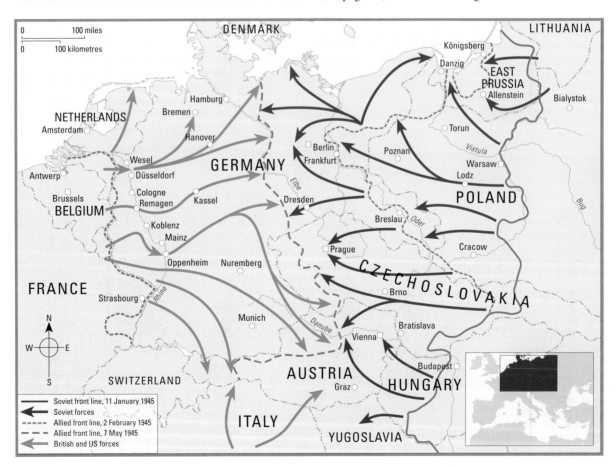

Germany was crushed between the Soviet forces advancing from the east and the Western Allies.

Hitler's last public appearance was in March 1945 when he distributed medals to members of the Hitler Youth movement.

immediate future of a conquered Germany.

On 12 January, the Red Army launched a massive offensive from the River Vistula, where they had halted five months earlier. They carried all before them, overrunning Poland and crossing into Germany by the end of the month, when their spearhead was only 65 km from Berlin. Further south, Soviet forces besieging Budapest in Hungary seized control of the city in mid-February, taking over 100,000 German prisoners.

ON THE WESTERN FRONT
On the western front, Allied troops reached the banks of the Rhine in the first week in March. The Germans destroyed all the bridges across the river well in advance of the arrival of Allied forces, except at Remagen where the Americans found a single bridge intact and crossed it on 7 March. It was another fortnight before further Rhine crossings were made, by Patton in the south at Oppenheim and, shortly afterwards, by Montgomery in the north at Wesel.

Germany's situation was hopeless. Poorly armed members of the *Volkssturm*, Germany's Home Guard, were drafted into the front line to reinforce its vastly outnumbered and outgunned armies. German roads were crammed with refugees fleeing westwards in front of the advancing Soviet forces. Hitler, now installed in

Survivors in Dachau camp cheer their liberation by the US Army on 3 May 1945.

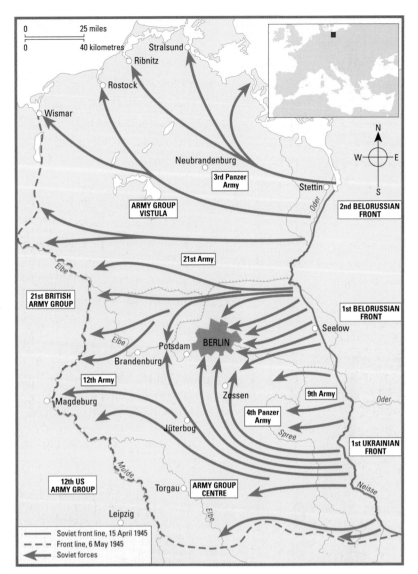

The First Belorussian Front, commanded by Marshal Zhukov, attacked Berlin directly from the east, while other Soviet forces joined in from south and north.

THE NATION WILL PERISH

Hitler was determined that if he was to go down, Germany would be destroyed with him. He gave orders to lay the country waste in the path of the invaders, saying: *'If the war is lost the German nation will perish. So there is no need to consider what the people require for continued existence.'*

[Quoted in *History of the Second World War*, B.H. Liddel Hart]

a bunker in Berlin, still clutched at straws. The death of President Roosevelt on 12 April was seized upon by the Nazis as a possible miracle that might save their skins – but Allied policy did not change.

Refusing to be drawn into a race with his Soviet allies, General Eisenhower decided to allow the Red Army to take the honour – and the heavy casualties – involved in the capture of Berlin. The Western Allies concentrated on mopping up in central Germany, accepting the surrender of over 300,000 German soldiers in the Ruhr in mid-April. On 25 April Soviet and US forces advancing from east and west met at Torgau on the Elbe River. By that time troops commanded by Russian Marshal Georgi Zhukov were fighting their way into the Berlin suburbs. The battle

raged from street to street ever deeper into the heart of the city. As the sound of gunfire drew near to his bunker, Hitler committed suicide on 30 April.

Hitler's death did not immediately halt the fighting, which stuttered on until ended by a series of separate local surrenders. In Italy Mussolini, who had been running a puppet government under German control since his fall from power, was captured by Italian partisans and shot on 28 April. The following day the German commanders in Italy signed an unconditional surrender. German forces in Berlin surrendered on 2 May – taking the city had cost the Soviets around 300,000 casualties – and the armies in north-west Germany followed suit on 4 May. Finally, on 7 May General Alfred Jodl signed a general unconditional surrender of all German forces, to take effect the following day.

WHEN THE FIGHTING STOPPED

Despite the vast scale of the war, it was not followed by any great peace conference setting out to redraw the map of Europe. When the leaders of the victorious Allies met at Potsdam, west of Berlin, in July 1945, the main item on the agenda was the still continuing war with Japan. Most questions regarding Europe were either settled according to agreements that had been made in the course of the war or resolved by whoever was in military control of a given place when the fighting stopped.

As they had agreed during the war, the Allies divided the defeated Germany into four occupation zones – American, British, French and Soviet. Berlin was deep inside the Soviet zone, but it too was divided between the four Allied powers, each occupying a sector of the city. Austria, once more separated from Germany, was similarly divided into occupation zones.

The western border of the Soviet Union remained what it had become in 1941, so the Soviets kept the gains they made early in the war, including the takeover of the Baltic Republics and of eastern Poland. In compensation, Poland was allowed to take land from Germany in the west – so Poland in effect physically shifted westwards. Otherwise, changes of borders in Europe were quite small. Czechoslovakia, Yugoslavia, Austria and Hungary were broadly returned to the shape they had been given after World War I – the largest change was that Yugoslavia took Istria from Italy.

American and Soviet troops meet at Torgau on the Elbe river on 25 April 1945. There was genuine warmth of feeling between soldiers of the Western Allies and their Soviet counterparts at this time.

The Soviet flag is raised over the Reichstag building in Berlin, 30 April 1945.

Nazi leaders on trial at Nuremberg in September 1945.

IMPOSING A SYSTEM

During World War II Stalin told a fellow communist: *'This war is not as in the past. Whoever occupies a territory also imposes on it his own social system. Everyone imposes his own system as far as his army can reach. It cannot be otherwise.'*
[Quoted in *Russia's War*, Richard Overy]

In the years immediately after the war, much effort was put into the 'de-Nazification' of Germany and the prosecution of Germans for war crimes (the Nuremberg Trials). The problem of German minorities outside the borders of Germany – the issue that Hitler had exploited so successfully in the 1930s – was settled crudely and brutally by driving them out of their homes. All the Sudeten Germans, for example, were expelled from Czechoslovakia. In total some ten million German refugees, who had fled or been deported from lands to the east, had to make new lives for themselves in Germany.

Victory in the war had carried Soviet armies deep into the heart of Europe. They did not go home for over forty years. The Soviet Union set about installing a communist political and social system in the countries under its military control – Poland, Romania, Hungary, Bulgaria and Czechoslovakia – while in Yugoslavia the wartime resistance leader Tito also established a communist regime.

The United States, under the leadership of President Harry S. Truman, was from 1947 committed to the task of resisting the spread of communism worldwide. The Americans took steps to prevent communist parties taking power in Western Europe, including funding the Marshall Plan, a programme to rebuild West European economies and thus encourage social stability. In 1949, through the North Atlantic Treaty Organization (NATO), the United States pledged to defend Western Europe against attack by the Soviet Union. Like the Soviets, the American forces had come to stay.

Because of the rift between the wartime allies, in Germany the military occupation zones solidified into a political divide. The American, British and French zones became West Germany (the German Federal Republic) and the Russian zone became communist-ruled East Germany (the German Democratic Republic). The Soviets tried but failed to force the Western powers to withdraw from Berlin by a blockade in 1948-9, and West Berlin was left as a western outpost deep inside East Germany. The dividing line between communist-ruled Eastern Europe and the West – a physical barrier of concrete, barbed wire, armed guards and minefields – was dubbed the 'Iron Curtain'. A durable legacy of World War II, the curtain was not lifted until 1989.

The results of World War II were by no means entirely negative, however. The experience of destruction on such a massive scale was a major motive for Britain, France, Germany and Italy to sink their old differences and become partners in the European Union and NATO. A war between them became unthinkable. Remarkably, the people of Europe and their governments really had learned a lesson from history.

By the mid-1950s, Europe was divided between a Western alliance headed by the United States and the countries east of the Iron Curtain dominated by the USSR.

The wall that divided Berlin from 1961 to 1989 – the most visible symbol of the division of Europe that followed World War II.

FIELD MARSHAL SIR HAROLD ALEXANDER (1891-1969)

Alexander commanded the British rearguard which held off the Germans during the evacuation of Dunkirk in June 1940 – he was the last British officer to leave France. In August 1942 he was appointed British Commander-in-Chief in the Middle East. He oversaw the victories in North Africa from Alamein to Tunisia, the invasion of Sicily and the Italian campaign. By the end of the war Alexander was Allied Supreme Commander in the Mediterranean.

GENERAL OMAR BRADLEY (1893-1981)

After distinguishing himself as a corps commander in Tunisia and Sicily in 1943, Bradley commanded the American forces at the D-Day landings in Normandy. During the campaign in Europe that followed, he commanded Twelfth US Army Group. His swift decision-making was to a large degree responsible for the defeat of the German Ardennes offensive in December 1944.

WINSTON CHURCHILL (1874-1965)

As a Member of Parliament in the 1930s, Churchill led opposition to Prime Minister Neville Chamberlain's policy of appeasing Germany. He joined the government as First Lord of the Admiralty at the outbreak of war

and in May 1940 replaced Chamberlain as prime minister, heading a coalition government including both Conservative and Labour politicians. In the summer of 1940 his policy of no-surrender carried the day against defeatists in the government and his defiant speeches helped sustain British morale. He travelled widely during the war, at considerable personal risk, to maintain personal contact with Britain's Soviet and American allies. Two months after victory in Europe, he was defeated in a general election.

GENERAL MARK CLARK (1896-1984)

Clark was US Deputy Supreme Commander, under Eisenhower, for the November 1942 landings in North Africa. He subsequently commanded the Fifth Army in the Italian campaign, from the Salerno landings in September 1943 to the German surrender in Italy at the end of April 1945.

GENERAL CHARLES DE GAULLE (1890-1970)

Before the war, de Gaulle was a modernizing French officer who vainly urged the French Army to adopt mobile warfare using tanks and aircraft. After fighting in the campaign of May-June 1940 in France, he fled to Britain and established the Free French movement as a rallying point for those opposed to the pro-German French government at Vichy. When France was liberated in 1944, de Gaulle headed a provisional government. Largely as a result of his efforts, France was recognized as one of the victorious allies in 1945, alongside Britain, the US and the Soviet Union.

ADMIRAL KARL DOENITZ (1891-1980)

Doenitz was appointed head of the German U-boat force in 1935. He masterminded the use of submarines in 'wolf packs' – coordinated groups hunting down merchant ships. Commander-in-Chief of the German Navy from 1943, Doenitz was chosen by Hitler to succeed him as German head of state, a position he briefly held until arrested by the Allies in May 1945.

SIR HUGH DOWDING (1882-1970)

Commander-in-Chief of RAF Fighter Command from 1936, Dowding played a large part in organizing Britain's radar-based air defences before the war. In May-June 1940 he resisted pressure to send too many RAF fighter aircraft to join the battle in France. During the Battle of Britain in July-September 1940 he made masterly use of limited numbers of men and aircraft to deny the *Luftwaffe* air supremacy.

GENERAL DWIGHT D. EISENHOWER (1890-1969)

Eisenhower was given command of the Allied invasion of French North Africa in November 1942. He proved so adept at the difficult task of making British and American generals work together that he was made Supreme Commander for the Normandy landings in 1944. During the subsequent campaign in Europe he was sometimes criticized for his cautious approach, preferring an advance on a broad front and refusing to race the Soviets to Berlin. After the war Eisenhower entered politics, becoming US President from 1953 to 1961.

REICHSMARSHALL HERMANN GOERING (1893-1946)

An ace pilot in World War I, Goering joined Hitler's Nazi Party in its early days in 1922. A powerful figure in the Nazi regime after 1933, he took a special interest in building up the *Luftwaffe*. In 1940 he boasted that the *Luftwaffe* would bring Britain to its knees. The *Luftwaffe's* failure dealt a crushing blow to his prestige. After the war, he was condemned to death at the Nuremberg War Crimes Trial but committed suicide before he could be executed.

GENERAL HEINZ GUDERIAN (1888-1954)

A leading tank expert in the 1930s, Guderian helped develop the Blitzkrieg style of fast-moving armoured warfare. His panzer corps played a leading role in the German victory in France in May-June 1940. Guderian led the 2nd Panzer Group in the invasion of the Soviet Union, but he was sacked by Hitler in December 1941 for withdrawing against specific orders to the contrary. Restored to favour, he was chief of the army general staff in 1944 when he again quarrelled with Hitler. He was on indefinite sick leave when the war ended.

AIR CHIEF MARSHAL SIR ARTHUR HARRIS (1892-1984)

Harris became commander-in-chief of RAF Bomber Command in 1942. He believed that bombing German cities would be a sure way of winning the war if only enough resources were devoted to it. After

the controversial bombing of Dresden in February 1945, he was criticized for having led a campaign that caused the deaths of hundreds of thousands of German civilians.

ADOLF HITLER (1889-1945)

As leader of the Nazi Party Hitler became German Chancellor in 1933 and Führer ('leader') in 1935. By 1938 he had effectively achieved total control over the German officer corps. In World War II he insisted on taking major military decisions himself. The swift successes of the first years of the war confirmed Hitler's view of himself as an infallible Man of Destiny. His subsequent mishandling of the war with the Soviet Union brought disaster on the German Army. After surviving an assassination attempt by German officers in July 1944, he killed himself in his Berlin bunker on 30 April 1945.

FIELD MARSHAL ERICH VON MANSTEIN (1887-1973)

As a German staff officer in the winter of 1939-40, Manstein suggested a new strategy for the invasion of France, in which the main thrust would pass through the Ardennes instead of through northern Belgium. He won backing for this idea from Hitler, who overruled the German High Command. The brilliant success of Manstein's strategy was matched by his skill in the command of troops in the field, both in the defeat of France and subsequently in the invasion of the Soviet Union. In March 1944 Hitler sacked him for retreating in the face of overwhelming Soviet forces. After the war Manstein was charged with war crimes and spent four years in prison.

GENERAL OF THE ARMY GEORGE C. MARSHALL
(1880-1959)

Marshall was US Army chief of staff from 1939 to 1945 – he took up the post on the day the war in Europe began. He energetically pursued the expansion and modernization of the US Army before America's entry into the war in December 1941. Once the United States was at war, he consistently supported the view that the defeat of Germany had to be given priority over the war in the Pacific. He retired from the army in 1945 and became US Secretary of State from 1947 to 1949. During that time he helped promote the recovery of Europe through the Marshall Plan. For this he was awarded the Nobel Peace Prize in 1953.

FIELD MARSHAL SIR BERNARD MONTGOMERY
(1887-1976)

After performing creditably during the disastrous campaign in France and Belgium in 1940, Montgomery was appointed to command the Eighth Army in North Africa in August 1942. The victory at El Alamein the following October made him a national hero. He fought in Sicily and Italy before becoming Allied Land Commander for the Normandy invasion in June 1944 and eventually leading Allied forces into northern Germany in 1945. A great believer in methodical planning and the crushing of the enemy through superior forces, Montgomery was often criticized by US generals for being slow and excessively cautious.

BENITO MUSSOLINI
(1883-1945)

As Italian dictator ('Il Duce') from the 1920s Mussolini claimed to be recreating the glory of the ancient Roman Empire – but he was privately well aware of the weakness of his army and his country's economy. In June 1940 he declared war on Britain and France, hoping to sneak advantage from a war won by Germany. A string of military disasters led to

his fall from power in July 1943. Rescued from prison by German paratroops the following September, Mussolini was set up as head of a puppet Italian government in northern Italy. In April 1945, he was captured by Italian partisans and executed.

GENERAL GEORGE PATTON
(1885-1945)

America's most inspired commander of armoured formations, Patton played a leading role in the fighting in Tunisia and Sicily in 1942-3. In 1944 he commanded the 3rd US Army in Normandy and in the subsequent breakout across France. In December 1944, his swiftness of response was crucial to the defeat of the German Ardennes offensive. Patton was, however, a controversial figure, nearly losing his command because of his aggressive attitude towards soldiers suffering from combat fatigue.

FIELD MARSHAL ERWIN ROMMEL (1891-1944)

Rommel performed impressively as a tank commander in the fighting in France in May-June 1940 and was promoted to head the newly formed Afrika Korps in February 1941. He generally outthought and outfought the British in the Desert War – earning the nickname the 'Desert Fox' – until the balance of forces turned overwhelmingly against him. Rommel had left North Africa by the time of the Axis surrender there in 1943. In command of the defence of

northern France at the time of the Normandy landings, he was badly wounded in an air attack on his car. Rommel was then implicated in the plot to assassinate Hitler and killed himself rather than be arrested.

PRESIDENT FRANKLIN D. ROOSEVELT (1882-1945)

President of the United States from 1933, Roosevelt was publicly committed to keeping America out of the war until his re-election to the presidency in November 1940. After that, he became increasingly open in his support for Britain. When the United States entered the war in December 1941, Roosevelt helped ensure that its major effort was directed against Germany, not Japan. Wartime summit meetings in

which he took part included ones with Chuchill and Stalin at Teheran in 1943 and Yalta in February 1945. At these meetings the leaders agreed, among other things, that a defeated Germany would be divided into zones, each occupied by one of the victorious powers; and that Poland's borders would change, with the Soviet Union taking areas in the east and Poland being compensated with German territory in the west. Roosevelt died on 12 April 1945. After the war ended, he was sometimes accused retrospectively of having 'delivered eastern Europe to communist domination', although it was never convincingly said what he could have done to prevent it.

JOSEPH STALIN (1879-1953)

As dictator of the Soviet Union, in the 1930s Stalin was responsible for the deaths of tens of millions of Soviet citizens, including most of the Red Army officer corps, who were executed in a 'purge' in 1937-8. His cynical non-aggression pact with Hitler in 1939 and his failure to prepare adequately for the

German invasion of 1941 brought his country to the brink of ruin. Yet between 1941 and 1945 he was able to motivate his people to heroic efforts through a mixture of patriotic enthusiasm and terror. Suspicious and cunning, Stalin mostly got the better of Churchill and Roosevelt in wartime meetings and he ended the war in control of eastern and central Europe.

JOSIP BROZ TITO (1892-1980)

Born Josip Broz, Tito was a Croatian Communist who organized a band of partisan resistance fighters soon after the German occupation of Yugoslavia in 1941. He won the backing of Britain and the United States who supplied his forces with arms and material, at the expense of rival partisans led by Draza Mihailovich. The Germans devoted some thirty divisions to the effort to suppress the partisans but failed. After 1945, Tito and his Communist party ruled the Yugoslav Federal Republic.

MARSHAL GEORGI ZHUKOV (1896-1974)

The outstanding Soviet military commander of World War II, Zhukov won Stalin's confidence by leading first the successful defence of Leningrad against the Germans in September 1941 and then the defence of Moscow in the following winter. He took much of the credit for the encirclement of the Germans at Stalingrad and for the Soviet victories of 1943 and 1944, and led the forces that captured Berlin in May 1945.

SIGNIFICANT DATES

16 MARCH 1935
Germany announces that it rejects the disarmament clause of the Treaty of Versailles.

3 OCTOBER 1935
Italy invades the independent African state of Abyssinia [Ethiopia].

7 MARCH 1936
German troops march into the demilitarized Rhineland.

17 JULY 1936
Beginning of the Spanish Civil War.

12 MARCH 1938
German troops march into Austria; Austria becomes part of Germany (the Anschluss).

29-30 SEPTEMBER 1938
The Munich agreement between France, Britain, Germany and Italy forces Czechoslovakia to cede the Sudetenland to Germany.

15 MARCH 1939
German troops occupy the Czech capital Prague.

29 MARCH 1939
General Franco, backed by Italy and Germany, wins the Spanish Civil War.

31 MARCH 1939
Britain and France promise to come to the defence of Poland if it is attacked.

7 APRIL 1939
Italy invades Albania.

23 AUGUST 1939
The Nazi-Soviet Pact is signed, secretly providing for Poland to be divided between Germany and the Soviet Union.

1 SEPTEMBER 1939
Germany invades Poland.

3 SEPTEMBER 1939
Britain and France declare war on Germany.

28 SEPTEMBER 1939
Invaded by the Soviet Union as well as Germany, Poland surrenders.

30 NOVEMBER 1939
The Soviet Union invades Finland, starting the Winter War.

12 MARCH 1940
The Winter War ends; Finland cedes some territory to the USSR.

9 APRIL 1940
The Germans invade Denmark and Norway.

10 MAY 1940
Winston Churchill replace Neville Chamberlain as British prime minister.

10 MAY 1940
Germany invades the Netherlands, Belgium and Luxembourg.

13 MAY 1940
German tanks enter France through the Ardennes.

26 MAY–3 JUNE 1940
Over 300,000 Allied troops are evacuated by sea from Dunkirk.

10 JUNE 1940
Italy declares war on France and Britain.

14 JUNE 1940
German troops enter Paris.

22 JUNE 1940
France and Germany sign an armistice.

JULY–SEPTEMBER 1940
The Battle of Britain: the RAF defeats the *Luftwaffe's* efforts to establish air supremacy.

SEPTEMBER 1940
Beginning of the Blitz – the nighttime bombing of British cities (continues to May 1941).

11 NOVEMBER 1940
British carrier-borne aircraft cripple the Italian fleet at Taranto.

11 FEBRUARY 1941
General Erwin Rommel arrives in North Africa to command Axis forces in the Desert War.

11 MARCH 1941
US Congress approves the Lend-Lease Bill to provide armaments to Britain.

6 APRIL 1941
German forces invade Yugoslavia and Greece.

20 MAY 1941
The Germans launch an airborne invasion of the island of Crete.

22 JUNE 1941
Germany invades the Soviet Union in Operation Barbarossa.

8 SEPTEMBER 1941
Leningrad is cut off from the rest of the Soviet Union; it remains under siege until February 1944.

5 DECEMBER 1941
Soviet forces launch a counterattack against the Germans in front of Moscow.

7 DECEMBER 1941
The Pacific war begins with the Japanese attack on the US naval base at Pearl Harbor.

11 DECEMBER 1941
Hitler and Mussolini declare war on the United States.

30 MAY 1942
The first 1,000-bomber raid against Germany is flown by RAF Bomber Command.

19 AUGUST 1942
Canadian troops raid Dieppe on the coast of Occupied France, suffer heavy losses.

13 SEPTEMBER 1942
The battle for Stalingrad begins.

23 OCTOBER–4 NOVEMBER 1942
The (Second) Battle of El Alamein: British-led forces defeat Rommel's Axis forces and drive them into retreat.

8 NOVEMBER 1942
In Operation Torch American and other Allied troops invade French North Africa.

31 JANUARY 1943
Germans surrender at Stalingrad.

13 MARCH 1943
German and Italian forces surrender in Tunisia.

5-14 JULY 1943
The Soviet Union inflicts another defeat on the Germans at the battle of Kursk.

10 JULY 1943
Allied troops invade Sicily.

25 JULY 1943
Mussolini is deposed as Italian head of government.

27–28 JULY 1943
An RAF bombing raid on Hamburg kills around 40,000 people.

17 AUGUST 1943
Sixty US bombers are shot down during raids on German factories.

8 SEPTEMBER 1943
The Italian surrender is announced; Allied troops land at Salerno the following day.

6 NOVEMBER 1943
The Soviet army recaptures the Ukrainian capital Kiev.

22 JANUARY 1944
Allied forces land at Anzio, south of Rome.

18 MAY 1944
Allied troops in Italy at last break through the Gustav Line at Monte Cassino.

4 JUNE 1944
Allied forces enter Rome.

6 JUNE 1944
D-Day: Allied forces invade Normandy.

21 JUNE 1944
The Soviets launch Operation Bagration, a major offensive that drives the Germans back into Poland.

20 JULY 1944
An attempt by German officers to assassinate Hitler fails.

1 AUGUST 1944
The Polish Home Army launches an uprising against the Germans in Warsaw.

1 AUGUST 1944
American forces in Normandy break through at Avranches.

24 AUGUST 1944
Paris is liberated.

3 SEPTEMBER 1944
Brussels is liberated.

17 SEPTEMBER 1944
Allied airborne troops are dropped into the Netherlands in Operation Market Garden.

16 DECEMBER 1944
The Germans launch a surprise counterattack in the Ardennes, beginning the Battle of the Bulge.

12–31 JANUARY 1945
The Soviets resume their offensive from the Vistula and push into eastern Germany.

4–11 FEBRUARY 1945
Stalin, Roosevelt and Churchill meet at Yalta.

13 FEBRUARY 1945
Soviet troops capture Budapest after a lengthy siege.

13-14 FEBRUARY 1945
Allied bombers destroy the city of Dresden.

7 MARCH 1945
American troops cross the Rhine at Remagen.

12 APRIL 1945
Roosevelt dies; Harry S. Truman becomes president.

28 APRIL 1945
Mussolini is killed by Italian partisans.

25 APRIL 1945
Soviet and American troops meet at Torgau on the Elbe.

30 APRIL 1945
Hitler commits suicide in his Berlin bunker.

2 MAY 1945
Berlin surrenders to the Soviet army.

7 MAY 1945
German commanders sign a general surrender.

8 MAY 1945
VE (Victory in Europe) Day.

airborne troops Soldiers carried into battle by air, either parachuting to the ground or landing in gliders.

annex To add territory to your country by occupying or conquering it.

appeasers Term used for British and French political leaders of the 1930s who believed that making concessions to Hitler would ensure peace.

armistice An agreement to stop fighting.

armour In modern warfare, a term for fighting vehicles such as tanks that are protected by metal plates.

armoured columns Large formations of tanks and other armoured fighting vehicles.

Aryan race According to the racist theories embraced by the Nazis, Aryans were a superior race of human beings, of which the German people were part.

beachhead An area on an enemy beach or shoreline captured by an invasion force, where more troops and supplies can be landed.

blitzkrieg In German literally 'lightning war' – a fast-moving offensive, especially using tanks and aircraft, designed to deliver a knock-out blow to the enemy as rapidly as possible.

coalition Term for a government made up of representatives of more than one political party.

collaborate In Nazi-occupied Europe, to cooperate with the Nazis and help implement their policies.

colonial authorities People running a country – a colony – that is ruled by another country as part of its empire.

Commonwealth troops Soldiers from one of the independent states once ruled by Britain, including Australia, New Zealand, Canada, and South Africa.

Communism Political and economic system of the Soviet Union, which spread to other countries after 1945. It favours a classless society and common ownership of property.

demilitarized Indicating a place where no military forces are allowed to be stationed.

democratic Having a government that is elected by the people and that allows a diversity of political movements and opinions.

disarmament Giving up some or all of one's weapons, usually by agreement between countries.

expeditionary force A term used in both World War I and World War II for the British troops sent to France at the start of the war.

front A place where hostile armies confront one another in a theatre of war.

guerrilla war War waged by lightly armed irregular troops, usually without uniforms, rather than the soldiers of a regular army.

Lend-lease program System by which the United States provided weapons and other supplies to its Allies in World War II without requiring immediate payment for them.

minorities Groups that differ in some way from the majority of the population in the society or country of which they are part.

mobilize To set in motion preparations for going to war

Nazism A system of government in Germany from 1933 to 1945, based on a belief in racial superiority and the rule of a strong and ruthless leader.

neutral countries Countries that do not take part in a war or give support to one of the warring sides.

OSS The acronym for the Office of Strategic Services, set up by the United States in 1942 to gather intelligence and carry out secret operations.

panzers German tanks and other armoured vehicles.

partisans Irregular troops fighting a guerrilla war.

partition The division of a country or area into different parts.

patriotic Referring to someone who is loyal to and supports his or her own country.

propaganda Information, often false or exaggerated, that is deliberately intended to promote a particular cause or to damage an enemy.

regime System of government; also a particular government or administration.

resistance movements Groups organized to oppose the government or foreign occupation forces in their country.

rout To beat an enemy conclusively.

sabotage The deliberate destruction of material, such as fuel, roads or bridges, to thwart the plans of an enemy.

salient Part of the front line which pokes forward into enemy-held territory, and so is surrounded by the enemy on three sides.

Slavs Inhabitants of countries in Eastern Europe, including Russia, Ukraine, Belorussia, Poland, Czechoslovakia, Bulgaria and Yugoslavia.

SOE Acronym for the Special Operations Executive, an organization set up by Britain in 1940 to send secret agents into enemy-occupied Europe.

SS *Schutzstaffeln*, an elite unit in the Nazi party, which also had its own armed troops – the Waffen SS.

theatre of war A geographical area in which part of a war is fought, e.g. 'the Mediterranean theatre'.

unconditional surrender The policy of the Allies, who decided that there would be no peace negotiations with their enemies – the enemy states would simply have to surrender without making any kind of peace deal.

Vichy France After Germany's defeat of France in June 1940, the French government that was prepared to co-operate with Nazi Germany moved from Paris to the town of Vichy; the area of southern France that this government directly ruled was called Vichy France.

Wehrmacht The German armed forces.

wolf packs Groups of German submarines hunting together for ships to sink in the Atlantic.

STATISTICS CONCERNING COMBATANT NATIONS

Casualties

Australia
Total 9,572	
Killed, excluding war against Japan:	Army 3,552
	Navy 903
	Air Force 5,117
Total killed including war against Japan:	27,073

Britain
Military killed:	Navy: 50,758
	Army: 144,079
	RAF: 69,606
	total: 264,443
Civilians killed:	62,974
Merchant seamen killed:	29,180

Canada
Total military killed:	42,042
	Army: 22,917
	Navy: 2,024
	Air Force: 17,101
Merchant navy killed:	1,148

France
Deaths:	
Military:	210,000 (of which 40,000 from Alsace-Lorraine fighting for Germans)
Civilians:	150,000 (bombings and resistance fighting)
Prisoners and deportees:	240,000

Germany
Military killed and missing (to Jan 1945):	Army: 3,269,000
	Navy: 149,160
	Air Force: 294,728
	total: 3,712,765
Civilian dead:	780,000 (estimate)

Italy
Some 150,000 army dead (including fighting for Allies); 50,000 naval and air deaths; perhaps 100,000 civilians died as partisans, in bombing, or after being deported

India (including present-day Pakistan and Bangladesh)
Total: 36,092 killed, mostly fighting against Japan

New Zealand
War deaths total:	11,671
Army:	6,839
Navy:	573
Air Force:	4,149
Merchant Navy:	110

South Africa
War deaths: total c.9,000, of which Air Force deaths: 2,227

Soviet Union
Total military dead: 8,668,400 (including 3.3 million died as prisoners of war)
Total civilian dead: 17 million (lowest estimate)

USA
Total US dead (all theatres of war):
Total dead:	405,399
US Army:	318,274
US Navy:	62, 614
US Marines:	24,511

Other European Death Tolls (estimates)
	military	civilian
Belgium:	12,000	76,000
Czechoslovakia:	10,000	215,000
Denmark:	1,800	2,000
Finland:	82,000	2,000
Greece:	79,743	350,000
Hungary:	200,000	290,000
Netherlands:	7,900	200,000
Norway:	3,000	7,000
Poland:	123,000	5,675,000
Romania:	300,000	200,000
Yugoslavia:	305,000	1,200,000

RECOMMENDED BOOKS

Of the many general single-volume histories of World War II, probably the best is John Keegan's *The Second World War*, first published in 1990. The war has given rise to many factual blockbusters, chunks of military history written to read like exciting action novels. Once the master of this genre was Cornelius Ryan, who in particular wrote *The Longest Day* (1959) on the D-Day landings and *A Bridge Too Far* (1974) on Operation Market Garden. Recently the leading author in this genre has been Anthony Beevor, whose *Stalingrad* (Viking 1998) was an international bestseller, and was followed by *Berlin: the Downfall, 1945* (2002).

SOURCES OF QUOTATIONS

African Trilogy, Alan Moorhead, Cassell, 1998.

English History 1914-1945, A.J.P. Taylor, Oxford University Press, 1965

Faber Book of Reportage, edited by John Carey, Faber and Faber, 1987.

History of the Second World War, B.H. Liddel Hart, Cassell, 1970

Hitler, Joachim Fest, Weidenfeld & Nicholson, 1974

Hitler Volume 2, Ian Kershaw, Penguin, 2000.

Russia's War, Richard Overy, Penguin, 1997.

The Holocaust, R.G. Grant, Wayland, 1997.

The Most Dangerous Enemy, S. Bungay, Aurum Press, 2000.

The Second World War: A Complete History, Martin Gilbert, Henry Holt & Co, 1991.

The Second World War, Henri Michel, Andre Deutsch, 1975.

RECOMMENDED FILMS

In some ways, the best films to watch on World War II are those made relatively soon after the war ended. They may be in black and white, with primitive special effects and some hopeless acting, but they capture the feel of the times. Such old movies to look out for include *The Dam Busters* (1954), *Dunkirk* (1958), and *The Longest Day* (1962), based on Cornelius Ryan's book mentioned above. As the war receded in time, movies about it tended to become gradually more cynical and harsh. Look out for *Patton: Lust for Glory* (1969), a biopic starring George C. Scott, *A Bridge Too Far* (1977) also based on Ryan's book, and director Sam Fuller's anti-heroic *The Big Red One* (1980), about the war as experienced by the US 1st Infantry Division. Recent movie-making on the war has been dominated by Steven Spielberg, with *Saving Private Ryan,* which uses modern special effects to give an impression of the terror of landing on the Normandy beaches, and the TV series *Band of Brothers.*

RECOMMENDED WEBSITES

The internet offers a vast archive of material both on the war in general and on every particular aspect of it. Starting points on the web might be:

www.historyplace.com/worldwar2

www.worldwar-2.net

Note to parents and teachers

Every effort has been made by the publishers to ensure that these websites are suitable for children; that they are of the highest educational value; and that they contain no inappropriate or offensive material. However, because of the nature of the Internet, it is impossible to guarantee that the contents of these sites will not be altered. We strongly advise that Internet access is supervised by a responsible adult.

PLACES TO VISIT

Among places to visit connected to the war in Europe, top of the list must be the Normandy beaches. Apart from the beaches themselves, Normandy is dotted with World War II cemeteries and museums. Of the many museums partly or totally devoted to the war it is especially worth mentioning the Imperial War Museum in London. A National World War II Memorial is due to open in Washington D.C. in 2004.

Numbers in **bold** refer to captions to pictures or, where indicated, to maps.